The Lisbon Massacre of 1506
and the
Royal Image in the Shebet Yehudah

Von dem chriſtelichen ſtreyt geſchehẽ
jm. M͞D. CCCCC. vj. Jar zu Liſzbona
ein hauͤbt ſtat in Portigal zwiſchen den chriſten vnd newen chri
ſten oder jūden/ von wegen des gecreutzigiſten got.

Von dem christenlichen Streyt: Edition B
by permission of the Houghton Library, Harvard University

HEBREW UNION COLLEGE ANNUAL SUPPLEMENTS

NUMBER 1

The Lisbon Massacre of 1506
and the
Royal Image in the *Shebet Yehudah*

Yosef Hayim Yerushalmi

CINCINNATI, 1976

Published with the assistance of the
Henry Englander — Eli Mayer Publication Fund
established in their honor by
Esther Straus Englander and Jessie Straus Mayer

Library of Congress Catalog Card No. 25–12620
ISBN 0–87820–600–0

Printed in the United States of America by
Maurice Jacobs, Inc.
Designed by Noel Martin

For
ALEXANDER ALTMANN,
Septuagenarian
In affectionate homage
Y.H.Y.

Contents

Foreword

This is the first in a projected series of *Hebrew Union College Annual Supplements*. The *Supplements* are designed to provide a medium for the publication of monographs, scholarly and desirable in every respect, but too long to fit into the *Annual* itself.

These *Supplements* are to appear from time to time, as material of appropriate size and quality in the Judaic field and the related area of the Ancient Near East becomes available. We shall strive to maintain in the new series the scholarly standards which, since its inception in 1924, have characterized the *Hebrew Union College Annual*.

We proudly present as the first in the series this searching analysis by Yosef Hayim Yerushalmi of the *Shebet Yehudah* and related documents, with his estimate of their implications for the history of Portuguese and Spanish Jewry.

June 1976   The Board of Editors

Prologue

This study began as an offshoot of work in progress on a new edition and translation of the *Shebet Yehudah* of Solomon Ibn Verga. Yet, while the focus is specific, the underlying theme can be traced through almost all periods of Jewish history. In its larger contours it concerns the persistent gravitation of Jewish political allegiances in the diaspora toward central authority, and the perceptions of this relationship on the part of the Jews themselves.

Jews seem to have learned early in their experience of exile that their ultimate safety and welfare could be entrusted neither to the benevolence of their gentile neighbors nor to the caprice of local authorities. It was natural, therefore, that in any given country or empire they should strive to come within the uniform jurisdiction and protection of the highest governmental power available, be it that of emperor or caliph, count, duke or king, bishop, archbishop or pope. They sought, in other words, a direct vertical alliance, even if this meant alienating lower officialdom, and was forged at the expense of horizontal alliances with other segments or classes of the general population. To speculate in retrospect whether the configuration might have been different is somewhat useless, since it assumes that Jews really had a viable alternative. The essential result, however, remains. In bypassing lower and local jurisdictions, Jews both gained and lost. If the central authority was prone to regard them as natural allies, by that very token they further aroused the resentment of an already hostile populace. The more the Jews sought the protection of the former, the more they found themselves in tension with the latter, and so each trend reinforced the other in a seemingly endless spiral. It was, on the whole, one of the more tragic aspects of the dialectics of Jewish existence among the nations.

The present monograph, then, could easily be telescoped both backward and forward in time, for potentially it is only one chapter in an as yet unwritten history of the alliance between Jews and the powers that ruled over them. The pattern is already fully manifest in the Hellenistic period, and remains consistent thereafter. Examples need hardly be multiplied here. We have but to recall that Alexandrian Jews placed their trust and loyalty, not in their native city, but in imperial Rome, and that the very earliest Jewish charters in medieval Europe established a direct and intimate link between the Jews and the Carolingian emperors which circumvented all inferior feudal relationships. These charters set both tone and precedent for the legal status of Jews in most European countries for centuries to come.

But our theme is not merely an echo of a dead past. Despite all other manifest differences, the modern era did not really effect a fundamental change in the dynamics we have sketched. Indeed, we would do well to take seriously the late Hannah Arendt's vigorous and proper emphasis on the extent to which Jews have allied themselves to the modern nation-state, have been identified with it in the eyes of other groups in society, and have therefore proved especially vulnerable whenever those groups became radically disaffected with the state itself. Equally pertinent are her observations on the frequency with which modern Jews have clung to an uncritical faith in the capacity and willingness of the state to protect them, even when such faith no longer bore any correspondence to reality.*

In the pages that follow I shall be concerned ultimately with Jewish attitudes and their consequences at a grave juncture in Jewish history. I trust the reader will understand why I have not confined myself to an analysis of events that are interesting and even dramatic in themselves, but have undertaken the more delicate and elusive task of uncovering what I have termed the "myth of the royal alliance" in the thought of Ibn Verga and others. Myth, in the sense in which we shall understand it, exhibits a vital historical momentum of its own, and here too a chronological extension of this investigation would reveal impressive continuities. If medieval Spanish court-Jews tended mentally to seat their sovereigns on too high a pedestal, their inflation of reality was later equalled, if not exceeded, by the adulation of various nineteenth-century Russian *maskilim* for Tsar Nicholas I.

I had intended, before releasing this study, to travel to Lisbon in hopes of garnering some additional documentary information from the archives of the Torre do Tombo. To my regret, the unsettled conditions in Portugal following the recent revolution have kept me from carrying out this resolve. I have not seen fit, however, to delay this publication further, and perhaps indefinitely. In sending it forth I am mindful of the despairing yet consolatory wisdom once expressed, I believe, by Paul Valéry: "A work is never completed, only abandoned . . ."

* * *

It remains for me to acknowledge some outstanding debts:

Several "generations" of doctoral students at Harvard have graced my Seminar on Sixteenth-Century Jewish Historiography over the last decade. Their queries, insights and arguments, have continually enriched and refined

---

*See Hannah Arendt, *The Origins of Totalitarianism*, 2nd ed. (Cleveland, 1958), especially Ch. 2: "The Jews, the Nation-State, and the Birth of Antisemitism." Cf. also Chs. 3–4, *passim*. On the Jewish alliance with the state in the Middle Ages see the general observations of Salo W. Baron, *A Social and Religious History of the Jews*, 2nd rev. ed., IX (New York, 1965), 135, and his *Ancient and Medieval Jewish History*, ed. L. A. Feldman (New Brunswick, 1972), Ch. 4 ("Some Medieval Jewish Attitudes to the Muslim State"), 83.

my own views concerning the *Shebet Yehudah* and a host of related topics.

My thanks to Professor Michael Meyer of the Hebrew Union College in Cincinnati for first suggesting this particular forum for publication, and for actively initiating the proceedings; to the authorities of the Houghton Library at Harvard, the British Museum, and the Bayerische Staatsbibliothek, for the use of their materials; to Carolyn Cross, for typing a difficult manuscript with her usual loving care; and to my student, Rabbi Marc Saperstein, for his prompt help in reading proof.

I am very grateful to Professor Sheldon Blank and the Editorial Board of the Hebrew Union College Annual for accepting this monograph to inaugurate their new series of Supplements, and to the two "anonymous" but unusually conscientious editorial readers whose helpful suggestions have been incorporated into the final text.

Harvard University
3 Adar I, 5736 — February 4, 1976

The Lisbon Massacre of 1506, and the Royal Image in the *Shebet Yehudah*

In April of 1506 the New Christians of Lisbon became the victims of a terrifying popular uprising. The massacre is described as follows in Solomon Ibn Verga's *Shebet Yehudah*:[1]

The slaughter that occurred there, in Lisbon:

I was out of the city, and when I returned after several days they told me that the two[2] are not to be compared, the only common factor being that it was evil and bitter in the extreme. And that which an old man related to me, that shall I write.

On Passover Eve the Christians found Marranos[3] seated before unleavened bread and bitter herbs, according to all the rites of Passover, and brought them before the king, who commanded that they be incarcerated in prison until the sentence be determined. At that time there was a famine and drought in the land, and the Christians gathered and said: "Why did the Lord do this unto us and unto our land, if not because of the guilt of these Jews?" And as their words were heard by the Order of Preachers who are called *Predicadores*,[4] they concentrated on seeking a device with which to help the Christians. So one of them arose in their house of worship and preached extremely harsh and bitter things against the seed of Israel. And they concocted a ruse and made a hollow crucifix with an aperture in the rear, and its front of glass, and they would pass through there a lit candle, saying that the flame emerged from the cruci-

---

(1) *Sefer Shebet Yehudah*, edited by Azriel Shohat with an introduction by Yitzhak Baer (Jerusalem, 1947), Ch. 60, pp. 125 f. All future references are to this edition. Still useful is the edition, together with a German translation, by M. Wiener (*Das Buch Schevet Jehuda*, Hannover, 1856; reprinted 1924). The book is also available in a Spanish translation by Francisco Cantera Burgos (*Chebet Jehuda*, Granada, 1924). For the older editions and translations see M. Steinschneider, *Die Geschichtsliteratur der Juden* (Frankfurt a. M., 1905), no. 90, pp. 78 f.

(2) Ibn Verga is apparently alluding here to the massacre both within Lisbon and in the surrounding countryside. On the latter, see our description of the events, *infra*, 15.

(3) Heb.: אנוסים.

(4) Heb.: פידריקאדוריש (*sic*), i.e., the Dominicans.

I

fix, while the people would prostrate themselves and cry: "See the great miracle! This is a sign that God judges with fire all the Jewish seed!"

A Marrano came there who had not heard these words, and he innocently remarked: "Would that there were a miracle of water instead of fire, for in view of the drought it is water that we should rather need!" The Christians, whose desire was evil, arose and said: "Behold, he mocks us!" That mob immediately took him out and killed him. When his brother heard, he came there and said: "Woe, woe my brother, who has killed you?" And one of the swordsmen arose, cut off his head, and cast him on his brother's corpse. After this all the friars arose and took out all the sticks of Jesus the Nazarene.[5] They went to the main avenue of the city and proclaimed: "Anyone who kills the seed of Israel shall be granted one hundred days of absolution for the world to come!" Then there arose men from among the mob with swords in their hands, and in three days they slaughtered three thousand souls. They would drag and bring them to the street and burn them. They would throw pregnant women from windows and receive them on their spears, the foetus falling several feet away. And similarly other cruelties and abominations which it is not worthy to recount.

Some said that all the Christian hatred was due to their hatred of a Jewish tax-collector named Mascarenhas,[6] because he was arrogant toward them and proliferated laws against them. Their proof is that as soon as they found Mascarenhas they ceased to slaughter.

The magistrates of Lisbon are not at all to blame, nor are its nobles and leaders, for all this was done in spite of them. They themselves went forth to save them, but because of the size of the mob they could not, since the latter almost laid hands on them as well, and they had to flee in order to save their own lives.

And the king of Portugal was a gracious king.[7] He was not within the city at the time, and when he heard, he wept and cried out against

(5) Heb.: עצי ישו הנוצרי—a pejorative reference to crucifixes.

(6) Heb.: מאשקארינייאש.

(7) Heb.: ומלך פורטוגאל מלך חסיד היה. The term *ḥasid* is not easily rendered into English. Depending upon the context, it can mean variously: "righteous," "benevolent," "charitable," "saintly," "devout," "pious," etc. In *Shebet Yehudah* Ch. 40 (p. 103) the pope refers to king "Pedro the Old" as "pious but not clever" (חסיד היה ולא חכם). Since the point of departure for this study is Ibn Verga's application of *ḥasid* to Manuel in the passage just quoted, I have thought it best to translate the word throughout as "gracious," with its implication of a grace that extends beyond the merely formal requirements of equity. The analysis later on of Ibn Verga's attitude to kings in general will, I trust, further justify this choice. Cf. also *infra*, n. 111.

the evil event. He came immediately to the city, investigated and discovered the plot of the friars, and intended to raze the house of worship from which the evil had emanated, but his courtiers would not permit him to do so. He intended to execute all the murderers, but the counselors showed him an imperial law that any crime committed by a mob of fifty people or more is not punishable by death, except for those who incited the evil. Then the king commanded that the friars be arrested, and he decreed that they be burned.

The city of Lisbon was called of old the Faithful City,[8] but the king decreed that for three years she be proclaimed the Rebellious City.

Students of the *Shebet Yehudah* have been puzzled by Ibn Verga's laudatory description of the Portuguese monarch as *melekh ḥasid* a "gracious" (or "righteous") king. It was, after all, this very king, Dom Manuel, who had ruthlessly ordered the forced mass conversion of all Portuguese Jewry less than a decade earlier, a tactic unknown among Christian rulers in the Iberian Peninsula since the days of the Visigoths. Moreover, Ibn Verga had himself been personally affected by the great tragedy of 1497. He was one of the many Spanish exiles of 1492 who had crossed the border into Portugal, only to be swept up five years later in the forced baptism of all the Jews of the realm. Living the dual life of a crypto-Jew when the pogrom occurred, Ibn Verga would seem to have had every reason to revile rather than extol the king who had compelled him and so many other Jews to abandon the religion of their fathers, and who had thus, by a combination of deception and violence, created the New Christian problem in Portugal in the first place.

The *Shebet Yehudah*, which Ibn Verga must have completed just before he finally succeeded in leaving Portugal, is an enigmatic work in other respects as well. We know all too little concerning the author.[9] The book itself is, at its core, an historical analysis of the causes of Jewish exile and tribulations

(8) Or—"Loyal City." Heb.: קריה נאמנה, a biblicism (Isa. 1:21,26) used by Ibn Verga as equivalent to the Portuguese title (*a mui nobre e sempre leal cidade de Lisboa*). Cf. *infra*, n. 41.

(9) For an analysis of the scant biographical information, as well as of the book itself, see Y. Baer, "He'arot ḥadashot le-Sefer Shebet Yehudah" (New Notes on the Book *Shebet Yehudah*), *Tarbiz* VI (1934–35), 152–79, and his aforementioned introduction to Shohat's edition of the text. Baer's conjecture that Ibn Verga ended his days in Italy, and that he completed his book there sometime in the 1520's, can now be dismissed. It has recently been demonstrated that Ibn Verga did leave Portugal shortly after King Manuel granted the New Christians permission to emigrate in 1507 but that he died in Flanders, probably en route to the Ottoman empire. See Meir Benayahu, "Makor 'al megorashey Sefarad be-Portugal ve-zeytam 'aharey gezerat RaSaV le-Saloniki: Genizat Sefer Ha-Emunot ve-giluyyo, ve-yediot 'al mishpaḥat Ibn Verga" (A New Source Concerning the Spanish

generally, and of the expulsion from Spain in particular. Yet problems of interpretation abound. Some of the most original and daring views expressed in the book are purposely veiled by being embedded in fictitious dialogues interwoven among the actual historical accounts of past persecutions. The book as a whole is ascribed by Solomon Ibn Verga to a forebear of his, Judah Ibn Verga, a deliberate if transparent attempt at pseudepigraphy. It was published posthumously by Solomon's son Joseph Ibn Verga, who added some new materials in his own name. It is not entirely clear, however, whether Joseph did not also wield an editor's pen even in places where he does not say so explicitly. The problem of extrapolating Solomon Ibn Verga's real views from the intentional ambiguities of the book is further complicated by the relative absence of ordinary controls. No other work by the author survives for comparison,[10] nor do we possess any early manuscripts of the *Shebet Yehudah* itself. While Yitzhak Baer has done important work in uncovering some of Ibn Verga's sources,[11] others are as yet unknown to us, or may have simply disappeared.

In view of these difficulties, Ibn Verga's account of the Lisbon massacre assumes particular importance for an understanding of certain key aspects of the book. It is, in point of chronology, the last historical episode he records. More important, the passage is virtually unique in describing contemporary events of which he had personal and immediate knowledge.[12] Even if he was, as he claims, outside the city during the pogrom itself, he returned to Lisbon within only a few days and so had fresh information on what had taken place. Fortunately, we also possess a fair amount of independent evidence concerning the massacre, as well as other statements on Manuel's Jewish policies written by Jews and gentiles. Hence, we are in a rare position to juxtapose Ibn Verga's account against these materials and, by drawing upon other elements in the *Shebet Yehudah* itself, to focus upon that which may be idiosyncratic or tendentious in his own interpretation.

Refugees in Portugal and their Move to Salonika after the Edict of 1506: Concealment and Discovery of the book *Sefer Ha-Emunot*, and New Information on the Ibn Verga Family), in: *Sefunot* XI (1967–73), especially 249 ff., 261.

(10) In *Shebet Yehudah*, p. 120, Ibn Verga refers to another work of his entitled *Shebet 'ebrato* ("Rod of His Wrath") which, if indeed it was completed, is no longer extant.

(11) Baer, *op. cit.*, as well as his earlier fundamental monograph *Untersuchungen über Quellen und Komposition des Schebet Jehuda*, Berlin, 1923.

(12) The only other explicit references to such events are his brief account of his own mission to ransom the Jewish captives of Málaga in 1491 (Ch. 64, p. 141), and the decree of João II to send Portuguese Jewish children to the island of São Thomé in 1493 (Ch. 59), at which time he was probably already in Lisbon. In a different category are his reports of the tribulations of the Spanish exiles abroad (Chs. 52–58), which are obviously derived at second hand.

The present study thus has two distinct but ultimately related goals. We shall closely examine all available data on the course of the pogrom which, though treated by other scholars, deserves a fresh review.[13] And, we shall attempt to relate this information to the *Shebet Yehudah* in order to see what conclusions can emerge from such an approach. The appendices will include the complete text of the very important contemporary German account of the massacre, based on three printed editions, two of them previously unknown, as well as the major documentary sources.

(13) The massacre of 1506 is discussed, *inter alia*, in the following works: Alexandre Herculano, *Da origem e estabelecimento da Inquisição em Portugal*, I (Lisbon, 1854), 142–56; English tr. by J. C. Branner, *History of the Origin and Establishment of the Inquisition in Portugal*, reprinted with a Prolegomenon by Yosef Hayim Yerushalmi (New York, 1972), 262–68; Meyer Kayserling, *Geschichte der Juden in Portugal* (Leipzig, 1867), 146–56; Heinrich Graetz, *Geschichte der Juden* (4th ed., Leipzig, 1891), IX, 209–14; S. P. Rabbinowitz, *Moẓa'ey golah* (Warsaw, 1894), 101–06; J. Mendes dos Remédios, *Os Judeus em Portugal*, I (Coimbra, 1895), 306–21.

I. *"The slaughter that occurred there, in Lisbon . . ."*

The forced conversion of 1497 had been a brutal act motivated solely by royal expedience. Under strong pressure from Spain to expel his Jews, Dom Manuel could not allow himself to do so. The Jews were apparently too important to the Portuguese economy and administration, and there did not exist a large class of converts who, as in Spain, would remain behind after an expulsion to continue the traditional Jewish economic and administrative functions. For Manuel, the only obvious way to rid Portugal of Judaism while yet retaining the Jews was to convert them all. Implemented despite considerable debate and misgivings in the royal councils, the forced baptism was rationalized by the hope that with the passage of time, and the gradual erosion of Jewish memories, the imposed faith would eventually be internalized and accepted out of conviction.

Though Manuel seems to have had no illusions concerning the Christian orthodoxy of the original converts, he was obviously persuaded that a genuine assimilation and integration could be effected. In the meantime, the New Christians had to be shielded from molestation and given sufficient time to adapt. To this end he issued his well-known protective edict in May of 1497 promising, among other things, that no inquiry would be made into their beliefs for the next twenty years. During that time he expected them to relinquish their accustomed habits, and to become habituated to the Christian faith.[14]

While Manuel was thus prepared to close his eyes to the lingering Judaism of the converts, he would not tolerate their emigration, for that would subvert the very purpose of the conversion. Royal decrees of April 20 and 22, 1499, forbade any New Christian to leave the country with his wife and children and, in order to render the sanction more effective, also prohibited anyone from selling bills of exchange to New Christians or buying immovable property from them. Otherwise the policy of toleration continued, and tentative steps were taken occasionally to bring the status of the New Christians into closer harmony with general Portuguese law. For example, on March 15, 1502, an old law of Afonso V concerning the inheritance of Jewish converts was declared applicable only to those baptized before 1497. All the rest were now to inherit in the same manner as Old Christians.[15]

---

(14) The text of the edict was published by João Pedro Ribeiro, *Dissertações chronologicas e criticas sobre a história e jurisprudencia ecclesiastica e civil de Portugal* (Lisbon, 1857), III, Pt. 2, p. 96; reprinted in Kayserling, *Gesch. d. Juden in Portugal*, 347 ff.

(15) For the edicts of 1499 and 1502 see José Anastasio de Figueiredo, *Synopsis chronológica de subsidios ainda os mais raros para a história e estudo critico da legislação portugueza*, I (Lisbon, 1790), 148 f., 158 f.

Still, this policy of *laissez-faire* did not have the desired effect. Coerced into an alien faith, the Jewish loyalties of most of the converts seem to have survived intact.[16] The cleavage between "Old" and "New" Christians remained as glaring as ever, not only because the Judaizing of the latter was notorious, but because in the eyes of the masses even their economic role and position in society were as "Jewish" as before. All the earlier accumulated hatred of the professing Jew was transferred to the baptized in a natural and direct continuum. Indeed, it was further aggravated by the very fact that the old legal barriers no longer applied to the convert, and that in his new status he seemed more elusive, and therefore more dangerous, than ever before.

The first serious outbreak against New Christians in Lisbon occurred on May 24, 1504. A group of them were insulted in the Rua Nova and, out of the altercation, a riot ensued. Forty young men who had participated in the attack were arrested, and the court condemned them to be flogged and banished to the island of São Thomé. Though the queen intervened and succeeded in having their exile revoked, the incident may be seen, in retrospect, as a harbinger of the calamity which was to come two years later.[17]

To anyone familiar with the dynamics of anti-Jewish massacres in the Middle Ages, the immediate background of the pogrom of 1506 betrays almost classic features.

Lisbon had always been subject to periodic outbreaks of the plague. In October of 1505 a new plague began in the city which was not to run its course completely until the end of April, 1507.[18] As was customary, the royal court moved on to other places. From Abrantes on March 11, 1506,

---

(16) The extent of crypto-Judaism among the Portuguese New Christians, as among those of Spain, has become a matter of lively scholarly dispute. It has been upheld, *inter alia*, by Y. Baer, I. S. Révah, and H. Beinart, and denied notably by B. Netanyahu and A. J. Saraiva. My own arguments in favor of the existence of widespread Judaizing in Portugal after 1497 need not be repeated here. They are presented fully, and with the pertinent bibliography on the current controversy, in my *From Spanish Court to Italian Ghetto* (New York-London, 1971), especially Ch. I, and in my prolegomenon to the reprint of Herculano's *Origin and Establishment of the Inquisition* (cited *supra*, n. 13). Some further bibliographic references will be found in H. P. Salomon's polemical review of the Herculano volume in *Journal of the American Portuguese Cultural Society*, VI–VII (1972–73), 59–65, 69–75. Cf. also Salo W. Baron, *A Social and Religious History of the Jews*, XIII, chs. lv–lvi, and XV, ch. lxv.

(17) On this incident see Herculano, *Da origem*, I, 139 (Eng. tr., 261).

(18) Damião de Góis, *Crónica do felicíssimo rei D. Manuel* (Coimbra, 1959), I, 229. The plague was also widespread in Spain, beginning as early as 1502 and reaching its peak in 1507. See the vivid account in Andrés Bernáldez, *Historia de los Reyes Católicos D. Fernando y Doña Isabel* (ed. Sociedad de Bibliófilos Andaluces, primera serie, no. 1, Seville, 1870), II, 295–99.

King Manuel wrote ordering a substantial evacuation of the city. He did so again on March 20. The victims were so numerous that on the same day another royal letter stipulated that two new cemeteries be created outside the city walls.[19]

Though the municipal council (Câmara de Lisboa) seems to have raised some objections, there is no doubt that a substantial evacuation took place.[20] One must presume that the nobility and the more affluent of the burghers found it easiest to make the exodus. The many citizens who remained in the pestilential metropolis were subject to all the inchoate fears and hysteria which similar situations have always engendered. To the horrors of the plague were added the sufferings of drought and hunger. Daily processions were held, the people clamoring for "water and mercy" from the Lord.[21] Still, even the plague could not close down one of the commercial hubs of the continent. Many foreign merchant ships were anchored in the harbor[22] and, as we shall see, their crews would play a significant role in the events that followed.

Though not reflected in the Portuguese sources, Ibn Verga's claim that the discovery of a Marrano celebration of Passover helped to further inflame an already volatile situation is independently confirmed in the dramatic and expanded account of an anonymous German visitor which was published shortly afterwards.[23] He relates that a group of New Christians who were celebrating the Passover Seder in a private home had been denounced to the authorities by one of their own. At 2:00 a.m. on the night of April 17,[24] a magistrate

(19) The text is printed in Eduardo Freire de Oliveira, *Elementos para a história do município de Lisboa* (Lisbon, 1882), I, 464n.–466n.

(20) Jerónymo Osorio states, perhaps with some exaggeration, that the majority of the residents departed (*De rebus Emmanuelis*, Coimbra, 1791, II, 162: "Maxima pars civium propter pestilentiam aberat").

(21) Bernáldez, *Historia de los Reyes Católicos*, II, 283.

(22) Damião de Góis (*Crónica*, 253 f.) speaks of "muita gente estrangeira, popular, marinheiros de naos q̃ entam vieram de Holãda, Zelanda, Hoestelãda, & outras partes"; Osorio (*De reb. Emm.*, II, 162): "Illis forte diebus multae e Gallia, Belgica e Germania, Olysipponem naves cum mercibus appullerant."

(23) *Von dem christenlichen streyt geschehen im MCCCCCVI Jar zu Lissbona, ein haubtstat in Portigal zwischen den christen und newen christen oder juden von wegen des gecreutzigisten got*, n.p., n.d. [1506]. For the complete text, and a discussion of the three separate editions of this pamphlet, see *infra*, Appendix A.

(24) *Von dem christenlichen streyt*, fol. 1r. On the basis of the German pamphlet, April 17 is the date for the Seder recorded by Kayserling (*op. cit.*, 146). Graetz, on the other hand, gave the date as April 8, 1505 (*Gesch. d. Juden*, IX, 211), and Rabbinowitz (*Moẓa'ey golah*, 102n.) noted the contradiction without being able to resolve it. However, in an addendum to the latter work (p. 382) the Russian Hebraist and mathematician Zebi Hirsch Jaffe proved conclusively that a) the year 1505 in Graetz must be an error (in that year Passover

and some constables suddenly broke into the house while they were seated around the table. Sixteen of the New Christians were arrested, while others managed to rush out and flee over the rooftops. In Abrantes the king was informed of what had occurred. Two days later the imprisoned were released. It was rumored widely, and plausibly, that their freedom had been obtained through bribery or the influence of highly placed persons. This brought about a feeling of general resentment. People said that the New Christians should have been burned.[25]

Almost all accounts agree that the immediate precipitating cause of the massacre that followed was an event which took place at the time in the Dominican Covent (Convento de São Domingos) in Lisbon. The convent contained a chapel devoted to Jesus in which, of course, there was a crucifix over the altar. As Ibn Verga reported, that crucifix became the subject of an alleged miracle, the other accounts varying only in their description of the visual details. Damião de Góis states merely that a "sign" was seen, while Jerónymo Osorio specifies that the crucifix contained an inlaid crystal, and that as the eyes of many were fixed upon it (as well, he adds, as their "imagination"), a light was seen to emanate from it. The most elaborate version is presented by the German who is, incidentally, the only chronicler to have actually visited the chapel during the height of the enthusiasm. He states that near the heart of the crucifix there was inlaid a mirror in which, it was said, Mary had been seen kneeling and weeping before Jesus. There were also many gilt stars in the crucifix, some of which lit up and waxed larger and smaller. At times two small lights were seen in the mirror; at others, a large thick one. Huge processions streamed continually to the convent to witness the miracle. Yet in a remarkably candid passage the German adds that when he was there he saw no lights at all, but was told by some two hundred people, as well as by good friends of reliable opinion, that the miracle had taken place. Whoever he may have been, he was sufficiently sophisticated

occurred in March), and that b) in 1506 Passover began on April 9, the first Seder falling on the night of April 8. (This information is repeated in Jaffe's notes to Rabbinowitz' Hebrew translation of Graetz's history, VII, 447).

Yet the date April 17 in the German account is quite reliable, requiring no emendation whatever. Jaffe simply missed the larger significance of what he had demonstrated. Not only are the two April dates reconcilable, they actually yield us a precious bit of information on Marrano life in Portugal a decade after the forced conversion. The point is, precisely, that according to the normative Jewish calendar Passover did begin in 1506 on April 9 (and ended on the 16th). But the crypto-Jews in Lisbon had apparently *postponed* their own celebration until the 17th, the day after the real holiday had ended, in the hope that this would help them avoid detection.

(25) *Von dem christenlichen streyt,* loc. cit.

to suspect, at least temporarily, that of which Ibn Verga was convinced. He states that he actually asked his friends if the miraculous phenomena had not been arranged artificially by the friars themselves. He was assured, however, that it was indeed a divine sign.[26]

He was obviously not alone in his scepticism. On Sunday, April 19, at 3:00 p.m., many people were present in the chapel to see the miracle. Among them were some New Christians. One of these "Hebrews recently enlisted in the ranks of the baptized" uttered a remark which, if not actually blasphemous, was interpreted as such. His precise words are variously given. According to Osorio he said that a miracle cannot happen to a piece of wood. De Góis has him say that a candle had been deliberately placed near the crucifix. In the German account he is supposed to have said: "How can a piece of wood work wonders? Take water and wet it, and everything will be extinguished!" It is hard to envision, of course, that he was so bold or so foolish as to make such deliberately biting remarks in the midst of the credulous throng, and it may be that what he said was really more innocuous, something akin to that which is quoted in the *Shebet Yehudah*. But it does not really matter. In such an emotional setting people heard, as usual, what they wanted to hear, and the crowd became enraged immediately. The German writes that it was the women present who were particularly infuriated. They dragged the unfortunate New Christian to the door, where they beat him until he lost consciousness, and then, joined by the men and some young ruffians, finally killed him. His body was taken out to the square before the convent and dismembered. When his brother arrived and demanded to know why he was killed, he was also murdered. A fire was kindled, and both bodies were burned.

Attracted by the commotion, the authorities attempted to intervene. A municipal magistrate arrived with many constables and attempted to make some arrests. But the crowd would not allow it, crying that since the king would not punish the New Christians, God must do so. When the magistrate insisted, the crowd turned upon him and forced him to flee for his life. They followed him all the way to his house and were about to burn it down, but in the meantime a general uproar against the New Christians had already begun in the city, and they left to join in the popular frenzy.

If, up to this point, the developments had been fairly spontaneous, the blame for the metamorphosis of a localized incident into a general massacre must rest with the Dominicans. Perhaps, given the conditions in the city, it would have happened anyway. But the fact is that the friars clearly took advantage of both the "miracle" and the murder in order to incite the entire

(26) *Von dem christenlichen streyt*, fol. 1r–v. For a completely different version of the miracle in a work by Jean Bodin, see *infra*, n. 42.

populace to riot against the New Christians. Indeed, throughout the ensuing days it was they who deliberately sustained the agitation whenever it showed signs of subsiding.

Immediately after the first New Christian had been killed at the convent, a friar arose in the pulpit to preach an inflammatory sermon against the "Jews." Meanwhile, two other friars took a crucifix (perhaps the very one which had generated the "miracle") and urged the crowd to murder with shouts of "Heresy, heresy...! Destroy this abominable people!" At the moment the magistrate's house was surrounded, thousands of men, women and children were already running amok through the city, slaughtering New Christians wherever they were to be found. Some were taken to the Praça de S. Domingos and there burned alive. Significantly, this plaza remained, throughout, the nerve center and focal point of the holocaust. Even when New Christians were killed elsewhere, their bodies would be tied with ropes and dragged here for burning. The German estimates that within the first twenty-four hours alone some six hundred New Christians had been put to death.[27]

Of the extant literary sources only the German pamphlet supplies information on that New Christian who, according to Ibn Verga, was the prime target of popular animosity. His full name is given here as "Johann Roderigo Maskarenus," obviously a teutonized form of João Rodrigues Mascarenhas, and it is claimed that he was "the head of all the Jews."[28] This assertion is both vague and exaggerated, and merely indicates that Mascarenhas was apparently one of the most prominent and powerful New Christians in the city. More concretely, Ibn Verga refers to him as *mokhes*, a tax collector, or tax farmer, but even this is not sufficiently precise, for there were, after all, various kinds of tax collectors in Lisbon. We do have an additional clue in the very fact that the German singles him out for vilification and states that he and his fellow Germans had "often wished fire and death upon him." Thus, not only the Portuguese but also foreigners deeply resented Mascarenhas, and this in itself would indicate that among his functions he was involved in the collection of customs duties from foreign vessels.

Concrete details are to be found, finally, in the receipt accounts of King Manuel.[29] Sparse as they are, they suffice to show that João Rodrigues Mascarenhas was indeed a person of considerable importance in the network

(27) *Von dem christenlichen streyt*, fol. 2r.

(28) "Johañ Roderigo maskarenus, der ist gewesen das haubt võ allen iuden." The account of Mascarenhas' fate occupies fols. 2v–3v in the German pamphlet.

(29) These have been published by A. Braamcamp Freire, "Cartas de quitação del Rei D. Manuel," in *Archivo Histórico Portuguez* (hereafter: *AHP*), vols. II *et seq.*

of royal finances, and that he maintained impressive and ramified financial dealings of his own. He was already in Manuel's employ by 1500, when he was in Castile on the king's business.[30] By 1502 he is referred to as the king's *escudeiro* (shield-bearer). Among his functions he is in charge of paying Manuel's household in his various dwellings (*moradias*), for which he receives the monies from the customs (*alfandega*), the Paço de Madeira, the wine-tax (*sisa dos vinhos*) and the inheritance tax of Lisbon, as well as the taxes of the Ribeira of Setúbal and the customs of Pôrto and Viana.[31] In 1503 we hear that for the past two years he has farmed the rents (*arrendamento*) of the Gambia River in Africa.[32] In 1505 he bought 6,000 *arrobas* (approximately 90,000 kg.) of the king's sugar from Madeira. Between 1504–06 he received the rents of the royal chancellery, and since 1505 he also had a contract for the 20% tax from Guinea (*vintena de Guiné*).[33]

The German reports that at the outbreak of the pogrom on Sunday, Mascarenhas had barricaded himself in his house "in a great street where most of the merchants lived," possibly the Rua Nova. When the mob arrived he stood at the window and hurled curses at them, threatening that they would all be hanged. They began to break into the house, but he had arranged an escape route over the rooftops, and fled.

On Monday afternoon he emerged in a place near that which is called

(30) *AHP*, V (1907), p. 74, no. 508. Cf. also *AHP*, III (1905), p. 158, no. 322.

(31) *AHP*, IV (1906), p. 72, no. 413.

(32) *Ibid.*, no. 414.

(33) These facts are revealed in three documents of 1509 settling accounts with his heirs (*AHP*, IV, p. 73, nos. 415–417). That the João Rodrigues Mascarenhas mentioned in these and in the documents cited above is identical with the Mascarenhas of the Lisbon massacre is clear from no. 417 which states explicitly that he died in 1506 ("e por elle fallecer o anno de 506").

Though a New Christian, Mascarenhas is never designated as such in the documents. Since he was already employed by the king in 1500, he was almost certainly born and raised a Jew and converted in 1497. However, his Jewish past apparently posed no obstacle in his rise to high office in the king's service. This is of some significance when we consider Spinoza's claim, echoed also by some modern historians, that, contrary to the Spanish practice, the Portuguese converts were excluded from honors and offices. (See Spinoza *Tractatus Theologico-Politicus*, in *Opera*, ed. Carl Gebhardt, III [Heidelberg, 1926], ch. III, 56 f.) It would be interesting to know whether Mascarenhas had already served the king prior to his conversion, but for this we would at least have to know his Jewish name. Genrally, of course, the Jewish names were exchanged at the time of baptism for Portuguese Christian surnames. An exception to the rule is an otherwise unidentified member of the Abravanel family, Henrique Fernandes Abarbanel, who appears in a document of July 20, 1509, as farming the rents of the Lisbon customs duties ("Amrrique Fernandez Abarbanell noso remdeiro d[e] Alfamdegua desa cidade"). See *Documentos do Arquivo Histórico da Câmara Municipal de Lisboa: Livros de Reis*, IV (Lisbon, 1959), p. 162.

"the little Jewry." It seems he had a horse waiting behind the church of Sta. Juliana, not far from the city gates, and was on his way there when four men accosted him and asked if he were unaware that everyone was looking to kill him. He offered them a thousand ducats or more if they would accompany him and enable him safely to reach the Church of Sta. María do Paraíso outside the city, where the Governor[34] of Lisbon was waiting with a force of four hundred men. To his misfortune, as they neared the Church of Sta. Juliana a young girl recognized him and raised the alarm. A woman approached, threw off his hat, and she too began to scream. Almost immediately, a crowd gathered and surrounded him. An argument developed as to whether Mascarenhas should be taken prisoner or killed on the spot. One man finally stepped forward and, declaring that unless he be killed forthwith he will manage to save his life, struck him a great blow on the face. This served as a signal for all to join, and though the four strangers would have protected him, it was useless even to try. Mascarenhas was beaten to death. As more people began to arrive they pounced on the corpse and stabbed it repeatedly. It was dragged to his house, which was now ripped apart and looted, and thence it was brought to the Praça de S. Domingos, accompanied all along the way by wildly exultant crowds.

The German had entered the city at noon on Monday in order to see what was happening, having presumably spent the previous day aboard his ship. His subsequent recollection of his initial reaction eloquently conveys some of the sheer horror of what he saw, all the more so when we consider that he was himself full of anti-Jewish bias and quite approved of what was taking place. The "great gruesomeness" (*grosser grawsamkeyt*) of the scene, he writes, would be unbelievable if it were to be told or recorded by anyone who had not seen it with his own eyes.[35] Three monks (i.e. friars), two of them Dominicans, were running through the city with crosses in their hands, yelling "Misericordia!" and "Death to the Jews!" They scattered in various directions, each followed by a huge throng, slaughtering and burning the "Jews" and looting their houses. Women, he notes, participated equally in the carnage. Further details are supplied by the Portuguese chroniclers. Bent on pillage, the mob entered the churches and there killed old people, children and young girls, who were clinging to the altars. Even those who merely "looked Jewish" risked death. Those who were known to have had dealings with New Christians were beaten. Often a gang of marauders would encounter some personal enemies in the street and, falsely calling them "Jews," would kill them before they had a chance to reply. The magistrates, Osorio says, did not have the

(34) "Der Gubernator," i.e., the Governador da Casa do Civel.
(35) *Von dem christenlichen streyt*, fol. 2r.

courage to quell the fury of the multitude, though Damião de Góis claims they tried, but were forced back.[36] Both assert that there were to be found some honest citizens who defended and hid some "Jews" from the mob.

Sailors from the foreign ships had joined in the pogrom almost from its inception. The German relates, in addition, that he and some of his countrymen (*wir theutschen*) had come to the Praça de S. Domingos and each contributed one hundred pfennig to buy more wood for the burning of the cadavers. When he arrived there he already saw two enormous mounds of burning bodies which he estimates at about four hundred in number. Now, just as the new wood arrived, the corpse of João Rodrigues Mascarenhas was brought in and burned upon it. It was, the German observes, money well spent. He and his compatriots were jubilant, for their oft-expressed wish that Mascarenhas should die had been fulfilled—*got sey gelobet!*[37]

Particularly important information is provided in the German narrative concerning the events of Tuesday, April 21, the third day of the pogrom. Not only do we find here the usual wealth of detail unavailable elsewhere, but the facts revealed can be used to obtain a new perspective on the entire affair. We shall confine ourselves for the moment to a recital of that which occurred, deferring an evaluation to the next section, when we shall integrate the data contained in official documents.

It was on Tuesday that the Governador da Casa do Civel and the Regedor da Casa de Suplicaçam[38] finally approached the city and entered into direct negotiations with its inhabitants, apparently through a large delegation whom they met outside the city walls. The governor issued a proclamation that all who remain faithful to the king should come forth and join the force of four thousand men he had brought with him. He further announced his firm intention to enter the city and punish all those involved in the rioting.

These fulminations, however, seem to have intimidated no one. The representatives of the mob protested that although they were ready to support the king in all his needs and rights, they must also be true to Christ and kill the Jews. For this, they said, they are prepared to sacrifice their lives. They threatened that if the Governor and his troops should "oppose the crucifix," they would actively resist him. Enraged, the Governor warned that if they

(36) Osorio, *De reb. Emm.*, II, 167: "Magistratus non tantum animi habebant, ut multitudinis furori se opponere auderent." De Góis, *Cronica*, I, 254: "E se hos alcaides, & outras justiças queriam acodir a tamanho mal, achavam tãta resistẽcia, que eram forçados a se recolher a parte onde estivessem seguros, de lhes nam aconteçer ho mesmo que ahos cristãos novos."

(37) *Von dem christenlichen streyt*, fol. 3v.

(38) The German account (*loc. cit.*) has "der gubernator und resator." For further details on these officials see *infra*, Part II.

14

continue to murder and loot they will be punished in their own persons and property. The crowd replied that they were prepared to stop looting, but they must destroy the Jews, and repeated once again that if the Governor, or any others, "proceed against the Cross," they will be killed.

At this juncture, if the German is to be believed, the Governor compromised. He told the people that they may go on killing the Jews, but they must not pillage anymore.[39] If these were indeed his words, he was obviously stalling for time and, pursuing the line of least resistance, attempted to limit the destruction of property in the city. Concurrently, he seems to have decided to go to the root of the trouble. He dispatched one messenger after another to the Dominicans, requesting that they return the crucifix to their church and cease to run about inciting the populace. They should try, instead, to calm the mob. If they refused, they must be aware that he had assembled a force, was awaiting additional men from the king, and would place them under arrest and hang them.

The Dominicans responded by rallying the people once more, urging them to fight the Governor's troops should any such attempt be made. In this they were supported. The Governor could only send the popular representatives back into Lisbon with the weak admonition that, even if his advice has not been followed, they should try to do "as little damage as possible."[40]

The Governor himself now entered the city and went directly to the Dominican Convent, but even his personal visit had no perceptible effect. Not only were more New Christians killed in Lisbon, but in the evening the slaughter spread into the surrounding villages where many of them had sought refuge. Peasants now joined with elements from the urban mob to look for New Christians wherever they could be found. Here, however, the Governor was able to act more resolutely. Though he had been reluctant to bring his forces into Lisbon, where they would have been outnumbered, he now led his men into the villages in pursuit of the marauders, and summarily hanged those who were caught.

Order was eventually restored in the city as well, though we shall yet have to consider how long this actually took. For our present purpose it will suffice to note that Ibn Verga's description of the punishment meted out by the royal wrath is, at its core, accurate. We shall see that the two Dominicans who had led the mob were indeed finally apprehended and burned at the stake. The inhabitants of Lisbon were punished and deprived of important privileges.

(39) *Von dem christenlichen streyt*, fol. 4r: "Ich bit euch ir wolt doch nit auff wolt horen, so geet hin und todt die iuden, stelt und rawbt nit, dan das golt und gut gehort dem kunig zu . . ."

(40) *Von dem christenlichen streyt*, fol. 4v.

Even the singular detail concerning the retraction of the traditional title of "Noble and Always Loyal" from the city's prerogatives is confirmed independently in Portuguese sources.[41]

In all, more than a thousand New Christians lost their lives, a catastrophe of the first magnitude.[42] Upon Solomon Ibn Verga the episode made, as we have seen, a profound impression. However, before we can comprehend the full impact of the pogrom in shaping his thought, we must first go on to review the events from a somewhat different perspective. We must inquire as to how King Manuel actually handled the crisis.

(41) E.g., Garcia de Resende, *Miscellanea e variedade de historias, costumes, casos e cousas que em seu tempo aconteceram*, ed. J. Mendes dos Remédios (Coimbra, 1917), no. 147, p. 53: "El Rey teue tanto a mal/ ha cijdade tal fazer,/ q̃ ho titulo natural/ de noble e sempre leal/ lhe tirou e fez perder." The relevance of this passage was already recognized by Kayserling, *Gesch. d. Juden in Portugal*, 153, n. 3.

(42) The estimates in the sources vary. The German reports at first that he has heard a figure of 1,930, and only subsequently adds that he believes it should be between 1,000 and 1,200. Osorio and De Góis both estimate 2,000, as does Christovão Rodrigues Açenheiro, *Chrónicas dos senhores reis de Portugal* (in: *Collecçao de Ineditos de História Portugueza*, V, Lisbon, 1824, 333). Bernáldez believes there were as many as 3,000 victims (*Historia de los Reyes Católicos*, II, 283). A Jewish eyewitness, Isaac Ibn Faraj (*infra*, n. 73), reports a figure of more than 1400.

Though of little practical value for a reconstruction of the actual events, it should be remarked that a somewhat vague and garbled account of the massacre of 1506 was also known to the famous sixteenth-century French political thinker Jean Bodin, and was used by him as part of an argument against forced conversion. In his *Colloquium Heptaplomeres*, completed around 1588 but not published until the last century, the character called Curtius recalls the Spanish expulsion of the Jews and the forced baptism in Portugal, and then continues: "When a meeting was being held in the capital of Lisbon, the wound of the crucified Christ which was painted red appeared to be flowing with blood when the light of the sun struck it. When a preacher saw this, crying out loudly he said: 'Look at the wounds of Christ the Savior, as they flow with blood.' The people in their amazement gave assent to these words. At this point a certain Jewish neophyte who pretended to be a Christian, in a loud voice rebuked the astonished crowd, saying: 'Why does that wood image of a dead man move you?' After the Jew spoke, the preacher bitterly cursed the man and his whole race as wicked and filthy because he lied with despicable deception that he was a Christian. The mob was incited by these words, and like mad men they dragged the Jew from the sanctuary and stoned him. Not content with this, the mob sought out the Jews everywhere in the city and killed about three thousand. When the king learned of this affair, he was gravely disturbed because he had forced the Jews to desert their own religion. And so he crucified the leaders of the uprising along with the preacher. (*Colloquium of the Seven about Secrets of the Sublime*, tr. Marion Leathers Daniels Kuntz (Princeton, 1975), 469 f. For the original Latin text see Jean Bodin, *Colloquium Heptaplomeres de Rerum Sublimium Abditis*, ed. L. Noack (Schwerin, 1857), 357, and Jacob Guttmann, "Über Jean Bodin in seiner Beziehungen zum Judentum," *Monatsschrift für Geschichte und Wissenschaft des Judentums*, XLIX (1905), 348.)

III. *"And the king of Portugal was a gracious king"*

All subsequent chroniclers are at one with Ibn Verga in declaring that, in one way or another, the king reacted speedily and efficiently to the riot, and that it was suppressed after the third day.

Osorio writes:

> As soon as D. Manuel heard the news of such notorious discords, he was inflamed by so violent a rage that he immediately dispatched Diogo de Almeida and Diogo Lobo with supreme authority to Lisbon, so that they give an exemplary punishment to these execrable deeds. A great number of the guilty paid with their lives the penalty for their madness and cruelty.[43]

Damião de Góis states that on Tuesday afternoon the Regedor Aires da Silva and the Governador D. Álvaro de Castro reached the city with the men they could recruit, at which time the fury of the mob was almost spent, since they were tired of killing and there was not much left to loot. And he continues:

> The news was given to the king in Avis . . . and he immediately empowered the Prior of Crato and D. Diogo Lobo . . . to punish those found guilty, of whom many were captured and imprisoned.[44]

Samuel Usque gives a brief summary of the massacre, and observes:

> If this catastrophe had continued, all the New Christians living in the city of Lisbon would have perished. But God's mercy arranged for the judges of the city to rescue them, *and then the king, who returned speedily from his quarters in the town of Abrantes*, aided them. Thus that fearful massacre ended.[45]

In reality, however, it was far from being so simple as these chroniclers, writing some decades later, would have one believe. They themselves tacitly admit that the pogrom raged for three whole days without any effective intervention on the part of the authorities. But beyond that, they have also compressed the actual course of events. The contemporary German account demonstrates clearly that the arrival of the Governor on Tuesday afternoon did not put an end to the rioting. On the contrary, in the evening it spread

(43) *De rebus Emmanuelis*, II, 168.

(44) *Crónica do felicíssimo rei D. Manuel*, I, 255.

(45) *Consolaçam as tribulaçoens de Israel*, ed. J. Mendes dos Remédios (3 vols., Coimbra, 1906), III, 31v; in Martin Cohen's English translation, *Samuel Usque's Consolation for the Tribulations of Israel* (Philadelphia, 1965), 205. Italics mine.

into the suburbs. Ibn Verga's own claim that the slaughter stopped with the death of Mascarenhas is an even more glaring exaggeration. We now know that Mascarenhas was killed already on Monday afternoon, which was but midway in the most violent phase of the slaughter. Furthermore, while we need not necessarily doubt that the climax of the pogrom had passed by the end of the third day, the carnage certainly continued for some days after, and it must have taken considerably longer to bring the city under full control. This is evident from the German pamphlet, still our most precise and reliable guide.

The German first reported from Lisbon (probably in a letter) on Wednesday the 22nd at the earliest, and possibly not until several days later, and it is significant that his report trails off literally *in medias res*. At this time he had heard that between fifty and one hundred people had been arrested, but he did not know what the king would do with them. He declares emphatically that the situation is still chaotic in and around the city (*es steet noch gantz wildt in Lissbona und umb Lissbona mit der gemein und dem pawrs volck ...*).[46]

Moreover, the chronicles, whether Jewish or Portuguese, have apparently not unfolded the full background of the uprising itself. Plague, hunger, hatred of the New Christians—all these played an important part in the final eruption. But its very dimensions, and the supreme difficulty which the royal authorities encountered in attempting to quell it, point to a deeper level.

A hint is already provided in the Mascarenhas episode. True, both Ibn Verga and the German make it seem almost a personal matter; Mascarenhas was universally detested. But why? He was, patently, a New Christian. At the same time he was involved in the collection of burdensome taxation. This suggests that the hatred which he elicited derived from more than his own highhandedness, and was symptomatic of a more profound unrest.

The vital link is provided unexpectedly from an outside source. In his *Historia de los Reyes Católicos* the contemporary Andalusian chronicler Andrés Bernáldez writes that, beside the factors already enumerated, there had been imposed on the city of Lisbon many bad *fueros*, favoring the king's rents and prejudicial to the interests of the community, and that it is because of this

---

(46) *Von den christenlichen streyt*, fol. 5r. At this point, in effect, the first printed report (designated by us as Edition A) ends. Nor does the German have anything substantial to add in his postscript, written as late as Wednesday, April 29, and included in Edition C (the date is stated explicitly). Here he only tries to revise his estimate of the number of victims. In a final addition, he notes only that the king has sent three powerful persons to Lisbon to apprehend the friar who ran about with the crucifix, but the latter has not yet been caught. For a discussion of the relationship between the various editions see our introduction to the German text, *infra*, Appendix A.

that the New Christians were so hated.[47] He obviously had in mind the recent reform of the *foraes* (as they were called in Portuguese), the ancient customary usages and privileges of Lisbon, which was begun early in Manuel's reign and completed in 1506.[48] Though various rationales were put forth for these measures, including the need to standardize the currency, the basic motive stemmed from the centralizing drive of the Crown. Under João II royal power had proceeded to consolidate itself at the expense of the nobility; now, under Manuel, it encroached upon the prerogatives of all classes. Always a tense and emotional issue in the Iberian Peninsula, any attempt by Manuel to tamper with venerable municipal privileges was bound to engender serious discontent.

Now if the population of Lisbon was particularly vexed by new provisions which, they felt, sacrificed their rights to the expansion of royal rents, and if, as Bernáldez affirms, this brought about a hostility toward the New Christians which exploded into violence at an opportune moment, it can only have been because the New Christians were themselves conspicuously involved in the same function they had performed as professing Jews prior to 1497, that is— they were often, like Mascarenhas, entrusted with the collection of the king's revenues. The Portuguese chroniclers of Manuel's reign did not mention the reform of the *foraes* as a factor in the Lisbon uprising because they wanted to present it exclusively as an issue between the mob and the New Christians, and not between the city and the king. They tried, as far as possible, to underplay the gravity of the revolt against the authority of the Crown, for that would hardly accrue to its credit. The thrust of their narratives is to show that the violence proceeded as far as it did only because Manuel and his court were away. Once the king was informed of what had occurred, order was immediately reestablished, and punishment swiftly meted out.

But we know now that it was not so, and it is perhaps no accident that our information on this score derived from two foreigners—a German and a Spaniard. We have seen that by Sunday evening, April 19, Lisbon was in complete anarchy, and that royal authority had utterly collapsed. From the very outset the king's officers were helpless. The murderers of the New Christian killed at the Convento de S. Domingos could not be arrested. On Monday, when the pogrom was at its height, even Osorio and Damião de Góis admit that the magistrates could or would do nothing. Most revealing of all are the events of Tuesday. Here, if there was any prior doubt, it is clear

(47) Bernáldez, *op. cit.*, II, 283f.: "... y había puesto en aquella Ciudad de Lisbona muchos malos fueros y condiciones en favor de las rentas del Rey y perjuicio de la Comunidad, y por esto los christianos querían muy mal á aquellos confesos y christianos nuevos ..."

(48) See E. Freire de Oliveira, *Elementos*, I, 377 f., n. 1; Figueiredo, *Synopsis chronológica*, I, 161 f.

that the massacre had passed over into full-scale rebellion. The Governor was brazenly defied and his own life threatened. The troops he had assembled were not allowed into the city. Had they made the attempt the result probably would have been open warfare. Lisbon was, literally, in a state of siege.[49]

And what of the king himself? Here we must glean what we can from the official documents available to us. We shall see that, far from conveying an image of decisive action on Manuel's part, they reveal throughout his considerable vacillation and procrastination.

When the plague first began in Lisbon Manuel had left the city to go to Santarem. However, the plague broke out there as well, and he went instead to Abrantes, where he resided for several months. He first received word of the pogrom as he passed through Avis on his way to Beja, where he was to see his mother Dona Beatriz who was gravely ill. Apparently, he was alarmed enough to cut short his stay at her bedside and go on to Évora, there to await further news from the capital.[50]

The first document at our disposal is a letter sent by Manuel from Évora and addressed jointly to four persons: Diogo d'Almeida, the Prior of Crato; Ayres da Silva, Regedor da Casa de Suplicaçam; Alvaro de Castro, Governador da Casa do Civel; and Diogo Lobo da Silveira, Baron of Alvito. The letter is dated Friday, April 24, 1506, that is, *five days after the beginning of the massacre*.[51] Regrettably, we are not in possession of the letters which must have passed back and forth in the interim, and so we cannot know just what steps Manuel had urged up to this time. From the letter at hand we learn that, whatever these proposals may have been, they had proved ineffective. The letter itself serves as further proof that the riot was far from quelled after the third day, and reveals the manner in which the king was attempting to cope with the still volatile conditions in the capital. Picking our way through

(49) Bernáldez (*op. cit.*, II, 284) is even more emphatic. He states that a "corregedor" succeeded in apprehending and hanging more than forty men, at which the populace was so enraged that they rose against him and hanged him in turn. Though this detail is not confirmed in our other sources, it cannot be ruled out. Even if it was only a rumor which Bernáldez received, it should be seen as a token of the seriousness of the situation. He also claims that the king was so outraged that at one point he threatened to destroy the entire city, but was dissuaded from doing so.

(50) Damião de Góis, *Crónica*, I, 255 f.

(51) First published in José Mascarenhas Pacheco Coelho de Mello, *Sentença da alçada que El-Rei Nosso Senhor mandou conhecer da Rebellião na cidade de Porto* (Pôrto, 1758), App. P, 120 ff.; Kayserling, *Gesch. d. Juden in Portugal*, 349 f.; reproduced *infra*, Appendix B, no. 1. [I should like to thank my colleague Francis M. Rogers, Professor of Romance Languages at Harvard, who deciphered this difficult Portuguese text for me with his usual facility after it had defied my own efforts. Any errors in the final translation which follows, or in the interpretation of the document itself, are mine alone.]

the convoluted syntax of the letter (itself perhaps a reflection of Manuel's indecision), we can abstract the following pattern of advice:

Manuel suggests, but does not really command, that one of the four persons addressed go to Setúbal and report there to the king's nephew "the Duke" on "everything that has happened and, what is more, is continuing to take place." (We shall see, further on, that the four were still outside Lisbon at the time.) This emissary is to bring to the Duke a letter, one of several which Manuel apparently enclosed on this occasion, telling him to go from Setúbal to Ribatejo, and to prepare from there to intervene directly. Another enclosed letter orders the preparation of ships in Setúbal and Cezimbra (the four addressees are to decide as to which particular ships), so that they may sail to Lisbon and there "force the entrance."[52] The salient feature of the letter is its complete lack of firmness, and the ambiguity of the assigned responsibilities. Thus, Manuel leaves it to the four to determine whether one of them will actually go to Setúbal ("if, in fact he goes"). Though the king thinks it "advantageous" for the Duke to come to Lisbon, *they* are to determine if the latter is really needed, or only the ships. For each alternative Manuel enclosed a separate letter of authorization, one of them marked "vessels." If the Duke does indeed go, the execution is to be "completely up to him"—in consultation with the four. If ships are to come from Setúbal without the Duke, Manuel seems to have enclosed two further letters to be given to two men of that town, instructing them to fit out their own vessels.

This, then, is the essential core of the letter. But only the text itself, with its qualifying clauses and second thoughts, can fully convey the hesitancy and lack of direction which make it an instructive example of bureaucratic ineptitude in a time of crisis:

Prior, Regedor, Governor, Baron, my friends: We, the King, send you many greetings.

It has seemed to us, after our having recently written to you through Pedro Correia, that because the things we bade you do in the matter have not been advantageous so far as the solution of that matter[53] is concerned, in addition to your informing us at once, one of you, namely, whoever might be the most available, should go to Setúbal and give to the Duke an explanation of everything that has happened and, what is

(52) The significance of this proposal is not entirely clear, though the route to be followed is obvious. Ships from Setúbal and Cezimbra would proceed through the Bahia de Setúbal, round the Cabo de Espichel, and then to the mouth of the Tagus River (Entrada do Tejo) leading directly to Lisbon. The phrase "force the entrance" would seem to simply the existence of a blockade, but we hear nothing of this in our sources.

(53) Port.: *união*, i.e. the matter of the uprising and massacre.

more, is continuing to take place, by means of this letter of ours which we have written to him, in which we recommend to him that, as soon as whichever one of you reaches him—if he in fact goes—he relocate himself and come at once to Ribatejo by whatever means appears best to him, in order to intervene in this affair either by force or by skill. Moreover, I am also ordering the fitting out and preparation of all the vessels of the said town, and of Cezimbra, which in the opinion of all of you should go, an opinion which that one of you who goes will take with him in the form of a message. Wherefore we inform you of the matter in this fashion, and we recommend to you that, in view of the fact that the affair has not been resolved, as has been said, one of you go to the said Duke my nephew and give him an account of everything so that he may come in the fashion we mentioned, and so that the vessels be taken care of as we mentioned, because it seems to us that it will be very advantageous for him to reach the city while we take care of everything else that is to be done. By the Duke's going in this way, we think it best that the execution of all the things which have to be done be completely up to him, in consultation with all four of you and taking note of your opinion and advice, and he will execute them. Wherefore, so far as this going of his is concerned, we think it best that it take place, provided it appears to all four of you that it is in our service for him to go. And if it seems to you to be so, then one of you will go, as has been said; and if in your opinion his coming is not necessary, and there is only need of the vessels, you will write to him to send the ones which seem to you should come from there, and you will send him our letter for him to carry out its contents. And you will write him the names of the people who in your opinion should come in them, so that everything can be made ready at once. If it seems to you that the vessels are needed to force the entrance, or to do anything which might be of service to us, in other words, if it seems to you that only the ships should come from there, then you will write him, and you will only send the letter on which "Vessels" is written. And if anything occurs to you, then one of you will go with the other letter mentioned above. And if vessels have to come from Setúbal, then send these two letters of ours to Simão de Miranda and to Nuno Fernandes, by which letters we recommend to them that each one fit out his own vessel and they come here with them to serve us in those things which you order them to do in our service. Written in Évora, April 24, 1506.

We have no information on the immediate results of the letter, whether one of the four actually journeyed to Setúbal, whether the Duke came, or if the ships were dispatched. The very proposal to bring ships is significant, a measure of the gravity of the situation. Above all, we begin to sense that the major difficulty lay in the cumbersome chain of command. The king was attempting to conduct everything from his seat in Évora. This meant that rather than issue orders directly, he had first, as in this instance, to obtain information from those who were in the vicinity of Lisbon, and then, in turn, to delegate them to make the immediate decisions and to transmit them to others.

Meanwhile, Manuel had also received a full report on the uprising from some of the highest municipal officials, to wit—the Corregedor, Vereadores, Procurador, and Procuradores dos Mesteres. On Sunday, April 26, we find him writing to these in reply.[54] Observing that the attack against the New Christians had been a great disservice to God and to himself, he declares that the inhabitants of Lisbon shall receive for this unaccustomed act his "very great displeasure." He will not permit such grave injury to his interests. Remedial measures which should have been taken and have not yet been effected must now be implemented.

The most significant disclosure in this letter is the fact that when the aforementioned officials first wrote to him they had stated that in order for everything to be corrected the king must personally come to Lisbon. This he flatly refused to do. He replied that since what had already occurred was irreversible, and considering the unhealthy conditions in the city, he is postponing such a step, confident that they already possessed more than ample means with which to cope with the situation. He therefore commanded them to join with the Prior of Crato, the Regedor, Governador, and the Baron, and together to take the necessary steps. He did not spell out what these should be. In a final display of bravado he added that if, perchance, the evil is so great that the city cannot extirpate it by itself (but of course he cannot believe that!) then he will not only come to Lisbon, he will enter it, even if the plague should become worse.

By the time this letter was dispatched, conditions in the city seem to have improved somewhat. Manuel wrote again the very next day (Monday, April 27) to the same men he had addressed on Friday.[55] He had learned from them that one execution had taken place, and that some arrests had been made by the judge João de Paiva. This has given him much pleasure. He congratulates them on the restoration of order, and the fact that justice has begun to be enforced without thereby provoking another disturbance. Punishment, he feels, even the death penalty, should be dealt out to those who deserve it, in particular

(54) E. Freire de Oliveira, *Elementos*, I, 395–401 (abridged in *Documentos do Arquivo Histórico da Câmara Municipal de Lisboa*, IV, 121). For the text see *infra*, Appendix B, no. 2.

(55) Mello, *Sentença da alçada*, App. P; Kayserling, *Portugal*, 350–53; *infra*, Appendix B, no. 3.

to the twenty or thirty women who, from what he has heard, were the original cause of most of the trouble. Still, he leaves all this to their discretion. If they feel that such punishments will lead to yet another uprising, they should so advise him, though he is inclined to begin as soon as possible. He recommends that they speak to the Vereadores, the Procuradores dos Mesteres, and the Vintequatro, and impress upon them their obligation to exert themselves in the capture and punishment of the guilty.

At this point, fully *eight days* after the fateful Sunday on which the slaughter had begun, we are considerably astonished to learn that those to whom this letter was addressed—the Prior of Crato, Regedor, Governador, and the Baron of Alvito—were still outside Lisbon. For Manuel goes on to say that if, in this work of justice, they should themselves have to enter the city, let them not hesitate to do so, since it is so important to his service and to the reputation of his state. They can stay at the Casa de Mina or in any other place. He has commanded Gaspar Vaz to gather his constables there, and they can make use of these as they see fit. He adds that he is also forwarding a letter to the Archbishop, summoning him to come immediately to Évora, whence he will send him on to Lisbon, since his arrival would do much to calm the clergy and the friars.

These details make one wonder if the king's felicitations on the restoration of order were not somewhat premature. And indeed, before completing the letter Manuel himself seems to have paused abruptly to reconsider some of what he had already written. Obviously worried over the potential consequences, he now advised, on second thought, that no punishment take place as yet. Let them first give him their opinion, and he will instruct João de Paiva to help in every way. He insisted only that the friars must be arrested forthwith and held in the castle, or in some other secure edifice. As for the New Christians—he had already commanded the addressees upon their departure from Évora to protect them. Apparently reacting to a suggestion that the New Christian survivors now be evacuated from Lisbon in order to avoid further incidents, Manuel replied that such an evacuation would not be in his interests. However, if the New Christians demanded to leave, let them do so early and by official order, so that their departure will not seem illegal. Also, they must not all exit together, for that may induce another riot.

Here the chain of available documents breaks off temporarily. We may assume that in the ensuing week the royal officials did regain an ever-tighter control in the capital, and that some of the more notorious ringleaders in the massacre were gradually rounded up and imprisoned. Manuel, to be sure, did not even then return to Lisbon, nor was he to do so until long after. He must have spent much of his time planning the precise manner in which he should punish, not only the perpetrators of the pogrom, but the rebellious city which had made a mockery of his authority and damaged his prestige. By May 3rd he appears to have decided on his course of action. On that day he wrote to the Vereadores Pero Vaz da Vega and Luis da Costa, as well as to the Procurador and the Quatros dos Mesteres, all of them members of the municipal council of Lisbon, and to its secretary Nuno Fernandez.[56] He ordered them to come immediately to Monguelas, and there to await his summons to present themselves before him in Setúbal, "in order," he states somewhat cryptically, "to discuss certain matters with you." We possess no record of the conversation. From the subsequent developments we may assume that the officials were informed of his firm intention to punish the entire city.

The full burden of royal retribution descended upon Lisbon in a decree issued by Manuel from Setúbal on May 22.[57]

In a preamble, the king alluded briefly to the slaughter and burning of the New Christians, perpetrated without fear of his officials nor of the penalties thereby incurred, and without considering how injurious all this was to God's service and his own. He stated categorically that the guilt devolves not only upon those who actually committed the crimes, but in large measure also upon all the other inhabitants of the city and its environs, because they failed to join actively with the forces of justice to oppose or apprehend the malefactors. Because the latter found no one to restrain them, their audacity increased, and the resulting evil was all the greater. Some people even allowed their own servants to run about without attempting to restrain or punish them. Consequently, all must now be punished according to the degree of their guilt.

The penalties were detailed in four essential clauses:

— In addition to their corporal punishments, all those directly involved in killing or robbing, as well as those who gave them aid and counsel, shall have their entire property confiscated.

— Those who did not participate at all, and yet did nothing to oppose the violence, shall have the fifth part of all their property confiscated.

— Upon publication of this decree and thereafter, there shall no longer be elected in Lisbon the *Vintequatro dos Mesteres*, nor their four *Procuradores*, and they shall no longer sit in the Municipal Council, all previous privileges notwithstanding.[58]

(56) E. Freire de Oliveira, *Elementos*, I, 401; *Câmara Municipal de Lisboa*, IV, 122; *infra*, Appendix B, no. 4.

(57) Damião de Góis, *Crónica*, I, 256–58; Kayserling, *Portugal*, 353–55; J. Mendes dos Remédios, *Judeus em Portugal*, I, 434 f.; *infra*, Appendix B, no. 5.

(58) The meaning of this clause will be discussed *infra*, pp. 28–29.

— Finally, the old vexatious usage of the *apousentadoria* was reinstated, whereby nobles, royal officials, and other powerful persons arbitrarily requisitioned the houses of burghers during their visits to Lisbon.[59]

It was, on the surface, a formidable document. Damião de Góis was sufficiently impressed to incorporate the entire text into his chronicle of Manuel's reign. And yet, its vigorous severity cannot obscure the king's earlier impotence in confronting the events when they occurred. In essence, Manuel exerted his full authority only after it had already been restored in Lisbon by his vassals, and by then it was too late for anything but retribution.

If, given the unusual circumstances, the tragedy could not have been averted, it would at least have been mitigated by effective action at the very outset. When first informed that the uprising had begun, Manuel refused to take the one decisive step which might have quelled the riot in time to save lives. His officials begged him to come to Lisbon, obviously convinced that only this could have any effect upon the mob. It was a legitimate request, warranted both by the gravity of the crisis and by precedent. In 1449, when a riot had erupted against the Jews of Lisbon, Afonso V responded to a similar plea by rushing from Évora to the capital and immediately ordering public executions to begin.[60]

But, as Manuel himself admitted, he feared the plague. Recently become a father (his son Luis had been born in Abrantes on March 3),[61] he refused to risk his life. The death of his mother may also have distracted him from his duty. In short, one may find certain extenuating circumstances, and we are not privy to his own thoughts at the time. Objectively considered, however, the primary failure was his, and one suspects that it derived, after all, from insufficient strength of character. His presence was required, but he would not budge. Instead, he contented himself with sending tentative suggestions

(59) The issue had cropped up repeatedly in previous centuries. On November 24, 1376 the king, D. Fernando, responding to the pleas of the Council, had forbidden the practice. Yet on April 22, 1383 he had to do so again in the most stringent terms. See the text of the decree in Oliveira, *Elementos*, I, 249 f., n. 1. In D. Manuel's own reign complaints had been voiced at the Cortes of 1498. See *Câmara Municipal de Lisboa*, IV, 34.

(60) Ruy de Pina, *Chronica de el-rei D. Affonso V* (Lisbon, 1902), II, ch. cxxx, 119 f.: "Foi El-Rei d'isto logo avisado por Pero Gaçalvez seu secretario, estando já com a Rainha na cidade d'Evora. E pedido com grande instancia, que a esta necessidade em pessoa quizesse prover, porque os rumores e alvoroços eram já taes na cidade, a que sem sua pessoa não se esperava resistir, á qual cousa El-Rei veiu em pessoa, e de muitos que pelo mesmo caso achou presos, mandou fazer publicas justicas, de que contra sua real pessoa se alevantavam oniões tão irosas . . ."

(61) Osorio, *De rebus Emmanuelis*, II, 161; Góis, *Crónica*, I, 246; Manuel's letter announcing the birth to the Lisbon officials, in Oliveira, *Elementos*, I, 394.

from Abrantes and from Évora, and thereby placed the entire onus for action upon his officials and the citizens of Lisbon themselves. Affecting a haughty disregard for the challenge to his own leadership, he shifted the issue and made it a test of the loyalty and zeal of his subjects in serving him. Upon such premises the entire blame could naturally be laid upon them.

And so it was. Damião de Góis informs us that the king later upbraided the Regedor and Governador for their "great negligence."[62] But while it could be argued that these might have acted more forcefully, on the whole they seem to have tried to do their best under the frustrating conditions which prevailed. The Governador, Álvaro de Castro, at least placed his own life in jeopardy when, on the third day, he ventured into the city to negotiate with the Dominicans. Throughout the week, if the royal officials could do little, it was because they had insufficient forces with which to operate and, above all, because they were not reinforced by the king's presence.

Characteristically, perhaps, such exalted persons as the Prior of Crato and the Baron of Alvito were not censured. Yet these men, and the nobility and high clergy generally, had done less than the Regedor and Governador. As late as Monday, April 27, the Prior and the Baron had still not entered the city in person. In fact, none of the august personages of the realm were as yet in Lisbon, and this was more than a week after the pogrom began. Why did Manuel wait until then to summon the Archbishop to the capital, when he himself was aware that the latter might help calm the friars? Why, indeed had he waited until April 24 before instructing his nephew to send more troops, and even then left it for others to decide whether the duke should actually accompany them? Clearly, no one of high station was in a hurry to go to Lisbon, and of course the king had not set the example.

All who had the good fortune to be away from the city during the riots, merely because they had already fled from the plague, were now automatically absolved. These were, presumably, the upper echelons of the Lisbon population, or at least those sufficiently affluent and leisured to have afforded a prolonged absence. Manuel's punitive decree of May 22 was directed solely against those who were physically present during the upheavals. In essence, it struck most heavily at the middle and lower classes and, despite the gradations in the penalties, affected the mass of the inhabitants. Such an unprecedented collective punishment of the capital cannot have been merely a response to the slaughter of the New Christians. However infuriated Manuel may have been at this brutal attack against a group to whose protection he was committed, his wholesale procedure makes sense only if we take seriously Bernáldez' contention that, whatever the immediate cause, this had been an outright

(62) Góis, *Crónica*, I, 256.

rebellion which ultimately derived from a deep-seated resentment of Manuel's recent policies.

This interpretation becomes all the more plausible if we focus on the third clause of the edict, abolishing the Vintequatro dos Mesteres, and barring their representation in the Lisbon municipal council. The significance of the step will become clearer if we examine the nature of this special target of Manuel's vindictiveness.

The *Casa dos Vinte e Quatro* (House of the Twenty-Four) was the elected governing body of the artisan class of Lisbon. Of ancient and obscure origins, the "Twenty-Four" achieved political power in 1383 when, in recognition of their support for his regency, the Master of Avis had brought them into the city government. In 1434 the number of those who were to sit in the Municipal Council was fixed at four, and this scheme persisted thereafter. Structurally, the arrangement was simple. All the artisans and craftsmen in Lisbon were traditionally organized into twelve *bandeiras*, or guilds, each of which annually elected two *homens bons* who together constituted the *Casa dos Vinte e Quatro*. These, in turn, elected from among themselves the four *Procuradores* who sat in the Municipal Council, and whose vote was required in any deliberation which affected the crafts in particular and the lower classes generally.[63]

By the time of D. Manuel the *Casa dos Vinte e Quatro*, its four delegates, as well as the *Juiz dos Vinte e Quatro*, later to be known as the *Juiz do Povo* (People's Judge) and also elected from its ranks, were the sole legal representatives through whom the popular will could normally be brought before the Council and the king. Indeed, in 1499 Manuel himself had ordered that in any municipal assembly only the Twenty-Four shall cast the vote representing the people.[64] By ordering the complete suppression of this institution in the wake of the events of 1506, the king effectively deprived the populace of whatever direct voice they had in government.[65] Though it is not actually stated in the edict, Manuel could presumably rationalize this drastic step as the penalty which the *Vinte e Quatro* must pay for their ineptness at the time

(63) On the Casa dos Vinte e Quatro see the general remarks of E. Freire de Oliveira, *Elementos*, I, 3–5, and especially the documentary study by Franz-Paul Langhans, *A Casa dos Vinte e Quatro de Lisboa: subsídios para a sua história* (Lisbon, 1948), itself an outgrowth of his earlier work, *As corporações dos ofícios mecânicos: subsídios para a sua história, com um estudo do Prof. Dr. Marcello Caetano*, 2 vols. (Lisbon, 1943–46). Unfortunately, most of the rich documentation concerns later centuries, with relatively little extant on the earlier period.

(64) E. Freire de Oliveira, *Elementos*, I, 384; Langhans, *Casa dos Vinte e Quatro*, lxx–lxxi.

(65) Of the scholars who have dealt with the Lisbon massacre, only J. Mendes dos Remédios (*Judeus em Portugal*, I, 315) noted the significance of the abolition of the Casa dos Vinte e Quatro. However, even he failed to appreciate the relation of this measure to the larger tensions between the king and the city.

28

of the riot. Perhaps it would have been idle to argue that none of the other authorities had been more effective. The point is that even if the Twenty-Four were thoroughly guilty, Manuel knew very well that the ramifications of his action extended far beyond an *ad hoc* punishment for what had actually happened. If the present incumbents of the office were really derelict in their duty they could have been removed and replaced by other men.[66] His decision to abolish the office itself, indeed the entire institution, was a blow against the fundamental privileges of the entire third estate in the capital from which all would suffer, even those who had not participated actively in murder and pillage. Though ostensibly a response to the pogrom, it would even affect some New Christians as well. Their preponderance in commerce should not obscure the fact that a fair number were themselves artisans and members of the guilds.[67]

Thus we see again how much more was at stake here than the issue of the massacre. Whatever Manuel's chagrin at the atrocities, it was the threat to himself which was now paramount. The entire edict of May 22 is suffused with one overriding theme—the rigorous assertion of his exclusive jurisdiction in Lisbon, and an enforced restitution to the damage done to his interests. The slaughter of the New Christians constitutes the immediate occasion, but no longer the essence, of the edict. Nowhere is there implied any compensation to the survivors for loss of life or property. All the confiscations went directly to the royal treasury.[68] In sum, not a pogrom but a revolt was being punished. The withdrawal of the honorific "Noble and Always Loyal" from the city of Lisbon was more than a symbolic gesture.

A few of the more notorious culprits were now sought out and punished. On May 28, a week after the promulgation of the edict, Manuel ordered all the friars but one to evacuate the Convento de S. Domingos and be dispersed throughout the province.[69] The two Dominicans who had sparked and sustained the riot, now identified as Frei João Moucho and Frei Bernáldez, an Aragonese, were arrested and taken to Évora. In July they were deprived of their habits and handed over, first to the ecclesiastical and then to the secular courts. Given the temper of the king, the outcome could hardly have been in doubt. The two were garroted and burned, their remains buried in the Monas-

(66) This is precisely what Manuel did in 1501, when he removed Afonso Dias from the office of Procurador dos Mesteres and ordered a new election (*Câmara Municipal de Lisboa*), IV, 83.

(67) Indeed, as we shall see, in 1512 Manuel was to stipulate that one of the four *Procuradores* of the *Casa dos Vinte e Quatro* must be a New Christian (*infra*, p. 33).

(68) *Infra*, Appendix B, No. 5.

(69) Pedro Monteiro, *História da S.ª Inquisição do reino de Portugal e suas conquistas* (Lisbon, 1749-50), II, 444.

tery of S. Francisco.[70] Of other executions we hear only that initially some forty or fifty persons were put to death. There is no evidence that such punishments continued for long.[71]

When all the aforementioned measures had been implemented, the problem of the New Christians remained. The massacre could not be brushed aside as a minor episode; it had radically altered previous perspectives. Above all, the optimistic hope which had been sustained since 1497 for a quiet and gradual assimilation of the Jewish converts had received a severe jolt.

The New Christians themselves did not now remain passive. They must have begun almost immediately to negotiate with the king for an alteration √ in at least one aspect of his policy—the prohibition to leave the country. In the aftermath of the trauma they had experienced, the demand to be allowed to emigrate must have been difficult to refuse. Even so, the negotiations continued for almost a year before Manuel finally brought himself to acquiesce. Perhaps he believed that by opening the gates he would be rid of the most recalcitrant judaizers, and that those choosing to remain would be all the more readily absorbed.

The decree was formally promulgated on March 1, 1507.[72] Manuel began by noting that, after the conversion of the Jews, he had forbidden all New Christians to emigrate without special permission. That prohibition was originally without limit of time and was implemented "for their own good." Now, however, he has changed his mind, and the restriction no longer seems necessary. Those New Christians who wish to remain in his realms shall be favored and well treated. As for those who wish to depart, since this is their desire it would indeed be better if they were outside his realms. Since the right of emigration has been requested by the New Christians themselves, and since he wishes to be gracious to them, the original decree is revoked. The new dispensation is now spelled out in a number of interesting provisions:

— All who want to leave for other Christian countries may do so freely, by land or sea, with their families and all their possessions, without any constraint or penalty.

— Those who do depart may return whenever they wish. They shall be favored and dealt with on a par with Old Christians.

(70) Christóvão Rodrigues Acenheiro [Azinheiro], *Chronicas dos Senhores Reis de Portugal*, in: *Collecção dos inéditos de história portugueza*, V (Lisbon, 1824), 333 f.

(71) "... y aunque después tomó el Rey su enmienda de algunos, fue de muy pocos" (Bernáldez, *Hist. de los Reyes Católicos*, II, 285).

(72) The text of this edict was printed from the original as one of the appendices to the law of King Joseph I, May 25, 1773, abolishing all legal distinctions between Old and New Christians in Portugal, and is reproduced *infra*, Appendix B, no. 6.

— The king also revokes the ordinances which had previously forbidden New Christians to sell their immovable properties for cash, as well as that which forbade others from making currency exchanges with them.

— He pardons all New Christians who had heretofore fled the country illegally. If they wish, they may return and settle in Portugal again. The only problem concerns some of the civil penalties they may have incurred. If, during their absence, the king has already granted the properties they left behind to other persons, the recipients thus favored shall continue to enjoy them by right, and the returning New Christians can only try to reach an understanding with them on their own.

— Those New Christians who have been ordered to deposit security against the possibility of their illegal departure are now relieved of this obligation.

— Manuel promises never again to legislate prohibitions against the New Christians as a separate group. They shall henceforth be treated in all respects like Old Christians, with no distinctions whatever.

— In a postscript, only one restriction is added: Those who desire to depart by sea must do so on Portuguese ships.

The consequences of this decree were profound. For many New Christians it meant a long-awaited liberation, and in the ensuing period a significant exodus certainly took place.[73] It is equally evident, however, that for a variety of reasons the majority of the New Christians chose to stay. We shall yet have occasion to reconsider this phenomenon.

Meanwhile, it remains for us to inquire into the subsequent course of Manuel's policies. Clearly, the king's harsh and repressive measures in the wake of the massacre of 1506 could not be prolonged indefinitely, and some mode of reconciliation had to be found. Already on October 24 of that year, following the intercession of Pope Julius II, Manuel allowed the dispossessed friars to be reinstated in the Convento de S. Domingos.[74] The edict of May

(73) In this connection see the vivid autobiographical fragment of one of the emigrants of 1507, Isaac Ibn Faraj, published by Alexander Marx, "The Expulsion from Spain: Two New Accounts," *Jewish Quarterly Review* (o.s.), XX (1908), 265–71. Ibn Faraj relates that his brother Meir had already fled secretly to Turkey in 1500, "though capital punishment was decreed by the king for every Jew who should leave the country without his permission." He himself witnessed the pogrom of 1506. In a harrowing passage he tells how, in the midst of the slaughter, he salvaged from the flames a part of the head of a close friend and kept it in order to give it Jewish burial later on. "Then the king allowed all the Jews to go to Christian countries, wherever they wished. After that, my brother and I went on a ship to Avlona, and then we came to Salonika."

(74) Monteiro, *Hist. da S.ª Inquisição*, II, 444 f.

22 against the city of Lisbon remained, at least on the books, for a full two years, but its revocation was quite foreseeable. Manuel could not afford to alienate his own capital for too long, especially when he stood in need of its assistance. That need arose in 1508, when the Portuguese enclave in Arzila in North Africa was besieged by the king of Fez. Manuel needed money and men from Lisbon. But his royal dignity, so grievously offended in the uprising of 1506, apparently required a loftier pretext before the punishment of the city could be formally rescinded. The simple solution was to ascribe the softening of the king's heart to the compassionate intercession of his consort. And so it was done. On July 14, 1508 the queen, Dona Maria, informed the municipal authorities of her successful intervention on behalf of the city, and urged them to present the necessary documents to the king so that the matter might be concluded.[75] On August 2, Manuel himself issued the edict restoring all the former privileges of Lisbon.[76] The preamble extolled the many past services of "our most noble and always loyal city of Lisbon," thus tacitly returning the forfeited title. For these reasons, and especially in view of the queen's affectionate request, the sentence imposed upon the city because of "certain negligences" (algumas negregencias) in the uprising against the New Christians is revoked, and all offices and honors reinstated.[77] On November 10, Manuel congratulated the city for its aid in the defense of Arzila.[78] The tension between the king and his capital was thus resolved, and it is therefore not surprising that, with the further passage of time, even the memory of the atrocities faded sufficiently to elicit a complete amnesty. On June 12, 1512 Manuel forbade any further prosecution for participation in the massacre, and halted any cases still pending.[79]

As for the Portuguese New Christians, no further outbreaks against them are recorded to the end of Manuel's reign. On the whole, royal protection seems to have been effective in securing the safety of their lives and property. Having allowed the emigration of New Christians since 1507, Manuel continued to pursue an active policy of integration toward those who remained.[80]

(75) E. Freire de Oliveira, Elementos, I, 403 f.; infra, Appendix B, no. 7.

(76) E. Freire de Oliveira, Elementos, I, 404 f.; Langhans, Casa dos Vinte e Quatro, 171; infra, Appendix B, no. 8.

(77) A comparison of this edict with the sentence of May 22, 1506 reveals that the latter did not mention certain penalties which are now removed. See the remarks of M. Caetano in Langhans, As corporações dos ofícios mecânicos, I, xxxvii f.

(78) E. Freire de Oliveira, Elementos, I, 407.

(79) Herculano, Da origem e estabelecimento da Inquisição em Portugal, I, 161 (p. 271 in the English tr.).

(80) E. Freire de Oliveira (Elementos, I, 299, n. 1) states, without citing his source, that in 1507 Manuel put an end to the special Jewish quarters of Lisbon ("as judiarias

A striking instance of his direct intervention in this regard occurred on May 6, 1512 when he commanded that one of the four *Procuradores* of the *Casa dos Vinte e Quatro* must be a New Christian.[81]

No doubt Manuel's promise in 1507 to dissolve all discrimination in law between New and Old Christians was also meant seriously. But his very need to intrude directly in order to secure a seat for them among the *Procuradores* is itself proof that "New Christian" persisted as a separate social category. Moreover, in certain sensitive areas, Manuel himself seems to have departed from his avowed policy and to have perpetuated even the legal distinction. An example of this may be seen in the printing of books. On February 20, 1508 the king issued privileges to Jacob Cromberger and other printers in order to promote the typographical arts, in which he stipulated that all printers must be Old Christians with no trace of Jewish or Moorish descent, nor suspicion of any heresy.[82]

Ultimately, Manuel's efforts at integration proved as unsuccessful as before. If he had indeed expected to rid the kingdom of its most volatile judaizing elements by allowing an unrestricted emigration, that objective was not thereby achieved. In retrospect one discovers that not all the New Christians who departed were Judaizers, nor were all who remained sincere Catholics. Still, Manuel apparently did not yet abandon his earlier hopes. On April 21, 1512 he extended for an additional sixteen years the twenty-year immunity from religious investigations originally granted the converts in 1497. But it seems that only a few years later he must have finally begun to concede that his policy of toleration was bankrupt. In 1515, abruptly reversing his prior assurances, he secretly instructed his ambassador in Rome to seek papal permission for the establishment of the Inquisition in Portugal.[83] For reasons as

fôram suprimidas por el-rei D. Manuel no anno de 1507"). The precise meaning of this is not entirely clear, except that it would indicate a further step toward integration of the New Christian population. What is quite astonishing, if Oliveira's assertion be correct, is the implication that for a full decade after the conversion of 1497 the Lisbon Jewish quarters, of which there had been two, remained intact and retained their "Jewish" character. The matter, like others, merits archival investigation.

(81) E. Freire de Oliveira, *op. cit.*, I, 10. This provision was subsequently revoked in the reign of João III when, by an *alvará* of Oct. 22, 1542, it was decreed that a New Christian cannot be received as a "filho da Caza dos 24" (Langhans, *Casa dos Vinte e Quatro*, 74, 177).

(82) "E mais que seram cristãos velhos ssem parte de mouro nem de judeu nem sospecta de algũa heregia . . ." (Figuereido, *Synopse chronologico*, I, 165). Cf. Venancio Deslandes, *Documentos para a história da typographia portugueza nos seculos xvi e xvii* (Lisbon, 1888), 12 f., and King Manuel II, *Catalogue of a Collection of Early Portuguese Books, 1489–1600, in the Library of His Majesty the King of Portugal* (Cambridge, 1929–35), I, 396 f.

(83) The text of the instructions sent to D. Miguel da Silva is published in the *Corpo Diplomático Português*, I (Lisbon, 1862), 355–59.

yet unknown, nothing came of this move at the time. The Inquisition was not to be introduced until well into the next reign, and even then, only after a prolonged and dramatic struggle. Yet although the establishment of the Portuguese Inquisition is naturally associated with D. João III, it must not be forgotten that he essentially implemented a policy initiated by Manuel. The "Fortunate King," architect of the forced conversion of Portuguese Jewry, was also the herald of that institution which would hound their descendants for centuries to come.

II. *"He came immediately to the city . . ."*

Having examined the massacre of 1506 and the policies of Dom Manuel in their several dimensions, we can finally consider the problem we posed at the very outset—the relation of Solomon Ibn Verga's narrative to the events themselves, as we now perceive them. For this purpose, however, it would be a futile exercise merely to juxtapose the account in the *Shebet Yehudah* against our own. Ibn Verga was no academic historian, and he did not even have access to the documents available to us. He described the pogrom as an involved contemporary, and from motives far different from ours. If we hope to focus on that which he suppressed or modified for his own purposes, we must single out from our discussion those details which we can reasonably expect him to have known.

Two serious distortions by Ibn Verga of the course of events are immediately apparent. Even if we accept his statement that he received his information at second hand from those who were actually within Lisbon at the time of the pogrom, he was surely aware that the slaughter did not cease, as he affirms, with the murder of Mascarenhas. He also knew very well that not only did King Manuel not come "immediately" to Lisbon; he did not come at all. In addition we may presume he knew that considerably more than three days elapsed before order was restored, and a much longer time before the city was punished. As a resident of the capital he would also have been aware of prior tensions between the city and the king.

But if Ibn Verga's account is selective in its disclosures and subjective in its interpretations, it is certainly not arbitrary. While inaccuracies both inadvertent and wilful are by no means unusual in contemporary Jewish chronicles, those that we find in Chapter 60 of the *Shebet Yehudah* assume a special character in light of the epithet *melekh ḥasid* which they are clearly meant to sustain. That the Portuguese chroniclers should approve the manner in which Manuel responded to the massacre is, after all, to be expected. But that Ibn Verga should employ such a glowing phrase seems almost shocking, and is in sharp contrast to the treatment of Manuel by other Jewish writers of the age. Abraham b. Solomon Ardutiel calls the king "the uncircumcised evil one." Abraham Zacuto terms him "Oppressor of the Jews," while Abraham Saba couples his name with the traditional cry—"May his name be erased!" For Samuel Usque, Manuel is quite simply the "Enemy." The Jewish chronicler Elijah Capsali, writing from the island of Crete, outdoes the others with a torrent of abuse. Manuel is "Bela son of Beʻor," "Pharaoh," "Haman," "The Worthless One."[84]

---

(84) Abraham b. Solomon Ardutiel, *Sefer ha-kabbalah*, in A. Neubauer, *Medieval Jewish Chronicles*, I (Oxford, 1887), 113; Zacuto, *Sefer Yuḥasin*, ed. H. Filipowski, 2nd ed. with

Nor do we find in Ibn Verga's curiously bland narrative[85] anything which approaches the sense of outrage so evident in the writings of Zacuto's brother-in-law, the apocalyptic mystic Abraham b. Eliezer Halevi. For contrast, one has but to read the latter's reference to the Lisbon massacre. He calls the Portuguese "butchers" (*kazabim* in Hebrew) and continues in a scathing and fantastic word-play:

> Its meaning is "those who cut".... But it can also derive from the verse "To the ends (*le-kizbey*) of the earth have I descended".... And this name (*kazabim*) is more fitting to the people of that sinful kingdom, the kingdom of Portugal, than to any other ... because there is not among all the families of Edom, nor among the other nations, one which will sail to the faraway isles at the ends (*be-kizbey*) of the ocean as do the men of Portugal....
>
> But they are also called *kazabim* because the Edomites [i.e., Christians] are butchers and cutters ... and though for this reason the name suits all the Edomites, nevertheless it is most appropriate to the men of Portugal because of the great curse and upheaval [they have wrought]. For they have devoured and confounded us, and decreed against all the Jews of their land harsh and evil decrees incredible to relate, and cut at will into their flesh. They were the butchers (*kazabim*), and the poor unfortunate Jews were the meat. And even later they became butchers in a literal sense against the Marranos ('*anusim*) who remained among

introduction by A. H. Freimann (Frankfurt a. M., 1925), 227; Abraham Saba's introduction to his '*Eshkol ha-kofer* on the Bk. of Ruth (Bartfield, 1908), 10; Usque, *Consolaçam*, III, p. 29v (202 in M. Cohen's English translation); Elijah Capsali's *Seder Eliyahu Zuta*, in the selections published by M. Lattes as *Likkutim shonim mi-Sefer De-Bey Eliyahu* (Padua, 1869), 83–87. See also Judah Abravanel's lament *Telunah 'al ha-zeman*, ed. Nahum Slousch, "Poésies hébraïques de Don Jehuda Abravanel," *Revista de Estudos Hebráicos*, I (Lisbon, 1928), 200, line 38, in which Manuel is called "a stupid king [מלך כסיל], fanatic in his faith, a hollow man." And cf. Joseph Ha-Kohen, '*Emek ha-bakha*, ed. M. Letteris (Cracow, 1895), 107, referring to Manuel as "this most bitter one" [המר והנמהר הזה].

→ A "King Don Manuel son of King Alfonso" also figures in *Shebet Yehudah* Ch. 12 as a protector of the Jews and, by extension, presumably also in Ch. 13 (beginning: "In the days of that king whom we mentioned above"). However, both chapters are so patently folkloristic, and so confused in the few historical facts they purport to offer, that they can have little bearing upon our study. Manuel was not the son of Affonso V, though he succeeded him to the throne, but of his brother Fernando. Ocaña, the ostensible setting of Ch. 12, is not in Portugal but in Spain. These and similar features will be dealt with more properly in my forthcoming edition of the book itself.

(85) Compared to the accounts in Osorio and Damião de Góis, both of whom convey the horror more vividly, and in greater detail, than does the Jewish author of the *Shebet Yehudah*.

them, and they brought their heads under the sword and killed many of them . . . And they are the ones who decreed various harsh decrees against Israel, as I have said, in order that the Jews bow down to their idols as they do, and their king is so devoted to his god that his thighs are permanently bent from the constant genuflexions which he makes before him.[86]

Even those sixteenth-century Portuguese writers who approve of Manuel's actions in 1506 express serious reservations concerning his implementation of the forced conversion of 1497.[87] It is therefore all the more astonishing that in the *Shebet Yehudah*, which describes the persecutions of the Jews through the ages and even includes many minor or localized incidents, the mass conversion in Portugal is not even mentioned! João II's deportation of the Portuguese Jewish children to São Thomé is recorded,[88] but not this far more decisive event. Such a blatant omission cannot be explained away merely by positing that Ibn Verga was ashamed to imply that he too was among the converted. Had this been his motive he would not have revealed that he was still in Portugal at the time of the massacre of 1506, a fact from which any contemporary would easily deduce what his fate had been. It remains a disturbing fact that in the *Shebet Yehudah* we encounter only Manuel the "gracious king" who swiftly punished the murderers of the New Christians, and hear absolutely nothing of Manuel the tyrant who, nine years before, had compelled the Jews of Portugal to be baptized.

To attempt to solve this apparent riddle, it is necessary to situate Ibn Verga's treatment of Manuel within broader contexts, taking account both of the historical experience of Sephardic Jewry in relation to the kings of Spain and of the general concept of kingship in the *Shebet Yehudah* itself.

Throughout medieval Christian Europe the Jews inevitably, yet willingly, allied themselves to the Crown as the best and, ultimately, the only guarantor of stability and security. Still, perhaps nowhere in Europe was this relationship more reciprocal, of longer duration, or operative on more levels of contact than in Spain. From the time of Alfonso VI up to 1492 the relationship was

---

(86) The Hebrew text was published by Gershom Scholem, "Ha-mekubal R. Abraham ben Eliezer Halevi," *Kirjath Sefer*, II (1925), 137. The verse cited at the beginning does not appear in the Bible in this form, but rather (Jonah 2:7) "To the ends of the *mountains* . . ."

(87) Osorio, *De reb. Emm.*, I, 51: "Fuit quidem hoc nec ex lege, nec ex religione factum. Quid enim? Tu rebelles animos, nullaque ad id suscepta religione constrictos, adigas ad cerdendum ea, quae summa contentione aspernantur & respuunt? Idque tibi assumas, vt libertatem voluntatis impedias, & vincula mentibus effrenatis iniicias? At id neque fieri potest, neque Cristi sanctissimum numen approbat." Cf. Góis, *Crónica*, I, 43.

(88) *Shebet Yehudah*, Ch. 59.

37

sustained by both sides, and regarded by Jews as a firm anchor through all vicissitudes. Again, though there were "court-Jews" and lobbyists (*shtadlanim*) in other countries, nowhere else did conditions favor the rise of so large and powerful a class of Jewish aristocrats, servants of the king and rulers of the community.[89] Rooted even earlier in the "golden age" of Spanish Jewry in the Muslim South,[90] it was this courtier class which forged the royal alliance into a central ideology. Conceived of in ultimate terms, Spain was of course *galut*, exile, and the advent of the Messiah was awaited and entreated. But until that time should arrive, the Jews of Spain placed their trust in the temporal monarchy and offered their wealth and energies in the service of the gentile kings of Castile and Aragon. It was the kings who gave the *aljamas* their sweeping and sometimes unparalleled autonomous rights, and who were the guardians of their safety. In the Jewish aristocracy's own relation to the Crown there was more than a grudging service. *Servi camerae* they may have been, but they were also the one group in Spain that worked heart and soul for the aggrandizement of the king and the increase of his power.[91] That the Crown could someday find it possible to dispense altogether with their

(89) On various aspects of the Hispano-Jewish aristocracy in Christian Spain see Neuman, *Jews in Spain*, II, Ch. 20; Y. Baer, *Toledot ha-Yehudim bi-Sefarad ha-nozrit*, 2nd ed. (Tel Aviv, 1965), 141 ff., 190 ff., and *passim* (also available in English tr., 2 vols., Philadelphia, 1961–66); Haim Beinart, "Demutah shel ha-hazranut ha-yehudit bi-Sefarad ha-nozrit," in: *Kebuzot 'ilit u-shekhabot manhigot be-toledot Yisrael ube-toledot ha-'amim* (Elites and Leading Groups: Lectures Delivered at the Tenth Convention of the Historical Society of Israel), Jerusalem, 1966, pp. 55–71.

(90) In this context see the remarks of Gerson Cohen in his edition and study of *The Book of Tradition (Sefer ha-Qabbalah) of Abraham Ibn Daud* (Philadelphia, 1967), p. xx.

(91) The point has been underscored by Américo Castro, particularly with reference to Alfonso the Wise: "The exaltation of the monarch's greatness was the work of the Jews" (*The Structure of Spanish History* [Princeton, 1954], 479). From what perspective Spanish Jews could view their "serfdom" to the kings is expressed succinctly in the dictum that through Divine compassion the Jews in their exile are "slaves to kings and not to slaves" (Isaac Arama, *'Akedat Yizhak*, Ch. 98 on Deut. 28 [ed. Venice, 1565, fol. 318b]; Abravanel, Comm. to Deut. 28:49). In commenting on Deut. 28:10 ("And all the peoples of the earth shall see that the name of the Lord is called upon thee, and they shall be afraid of thee"), the 14th century exegete Bahya b. Asher of Saragossa offers this analogy: "He who is a servant of one of the king's nobles is not of such high station as though he were servant of the king, for the servant of the king is feared even by the nobles and ministers out of fear of the king himself, since that servant is called by the name of the king their master" (*Be'ur 'al ha-Torah*, ed. C. B. Chavel [Jerusalem, 1968], III, 423). For a sketch of the relations between Spanish Jewry and the kings, see Neuman, *Jews in Spain*, I, Ch. I. It is no less characteristic than ironic that in 1492 the Spanish Jewish communities celebrated the Christian conquest of Granada with considerable enthusiasm (see Haim Hillel Ben-Sasson, "Dor goley Sefarad 'al 'azmo" [The Generation of the Spanish Exiles on its Fate], *Zion*, XXVI [1961], 26 f.).

services must have been inconceivable; the assumed identity of interest between king and Jews was to them axiomatic. To say merely that the Jews of
Spain had no other choice but to cast their lot entirely with their sovereigns
is to state a truth, and yet to miss the point. Born of necessity, confirmed by
history, the royal alliance flowered beyond its obvious mundane realities into
a guiding myth which gripped many of the Hispano-Jewish elite down to the
very eve of the Expulsion.

Though it can be documented from Spanish-Jewish literature over the
centuries, the very quintessence of that myth is distilled, as it were, in the
pages of the *Shebet Yehudah*. What makes Ibn Verga's panegyric of kingship
especially instructive is that it comes *after* the Expulsion and that it is gen-
eralized to *all* kings, even those of other countries. The benevolence of kings
to their Jews becomes, in the *Shebet Yehudah*, a universal principle. The extent
to which Ibn Verga is willing to apply it becomes evident when we examine
the book.

In Ibn Verga's eyes, kings, and royal officials generally, are always ardent
protectors of the Jews against the attacks of the rabble. When the Jews are
not saved, it is not for lack of royal will, but because of the obstinacy and
power of the *vulgus*. To be sure, this was often enough the case in medieval
Europe, and some of the examples cited are historically unimpeachable. Thus,
in a classic instance, during the Shepherd Massacres of 1321 the Senéschal of
Toulouse, delegated representative of the King of France, repeatedly exerts
himself to save the local Jews but is prevented from doing so by the inflamed
populace.[92] In other chapters, however, Ibn Verga freely invents or elabo-
rates in order to score his point. During the Black Death the Jews are accused
of poisoning the rivers, and Ibn Verga has an unidentified king try to prove
the absurdity of the charge, only to be thwarted in the end by the insistence
of the mob.[93] In Southern Italy in 1290 a priest accuses the Jews of desecrating
a cross. The people are incited to a massacre, and, unable to save them, the
royal officials advise their conversion. According to Ibn Verga, when the king
wished to hang the priest the people opposed him, and he had to content

(92) *Shebet Yehudah*, Ch. 6. Ibn Verga's account is strikingly confirmed by the testimony of Barukh, a German Jew forcibly converted in Toulouse at the time of the massacre,
when he was tried by the Inquisition for relapse into Judaism. The Latin protocol was
published by Jean-Marie Vidal, "Déposition du juif Baruc devant l'Inquisition de Pamiers,"
Annales de St. Louis-des-Français, III–IV (1898–1900), 154–74, and translated into English
by Solomon Grayzel, "The Confession of a Medieval Jewish Convert," *Historia Judaica*,
XVII (1955), 89–120.

(93) *Shebet Yehudah*, Ch. 26. Ibn Verga's source is not known. In Usque's account
of the Black Death no such treatment is accorded the king. See *Consolaçam*, III, 20v;
ed. Cohen, 192.

39

himself with ordering banishment instead.[94] In what is perhaps the most revealing passage of all, Ibn Verga presents a singular interpretation of the expulsion from England. Though he shows himself aware of the fact that the Jews were accused of clipping the coinage, he goes on to write that the king discovered the accusation to be false, and that he expelled them only for fear of the mob and against his own better judgment![95]

Equally significant are the words that Ibn Verga chooses to place in the mouth of the fictional "Alfonso," who serves in the book as a model of an enlightened Spanish king, when the people accuse the Jews of ritual murder. To "Tomás," a similar prototype of a Christian savant, the king confides:

> Six days ago there came to our place a servant of our Savior, a certain bishop, and he preached publicly that the Jews cannot celebrate a festival called *Pesaḥ* in the Hebrew tongue, except with Christian blood. Now although I have seen in that man more marks of foolishness than of wisdom, what shall I do? The people have believed his words and have come to demand judgement, trampling my courtyards! Since that error has been confirmed as true in their polluted minds, I have appeared to them as an alien or a Jew, because I have taken no revenge against the Jews. Though this thing is absolutely removed from reason, I should like to know what to reply to the fools, for they are many, and I cannot easily dissuade them. . . . If there be in the Jews such a sin, I will expel them from my land. But if it be a lie, I shall risk my life to save them, for they are my servants.[96]

(94) *Shebet Yehudah*, Ch. 19. No extant source.

(95) *Shebet Yehudah*, Ch. 18. Cf. the quotation from Profiat Duran's lost chronicle *Zikhron ha-shemadot* cited by Isaac Abravanel, *Yeshu'ot Meshiḥo* (Koenigsberg, 1861), 46r, and Usque, *Consolaçam*, III, 11v–13r (ed. Cohen, 180 ff.) where, though the clipping of the coins is also stressed, there are no attempts to place the king in a favorable light. The tendentious purpose of Ibn Verga's invention has been noted by A. Shohat (p. 185, *ad loc.*).

(96) *Shebet Yehudah*, Ch. 7, p. 26. For all the king's basic good will and firm desire to protect the Jews, note that he is not altogether certain that the charge may not have some substance. Indeed, in another ritual murder libel reported in Ch. 29 (p. 72) "the upright old King Alfonso," though initially skeptical, is persuaded by the testimony of false witnesses to have an accused Jew put to the torture. The king is brought back to good sense only when an enlightened bishop persuades him of the futility of extracting confessions under duress. Thus, even "gracious" and "upright" kings are sometimes susceptible to ritual murder propaganda. While the Alfonso who appears in the *Shebet Yehudah* is not to be identified with any one historical figure, one wonders if Ibn Verga was not aware that in the great legal code compiled under the aegis of Alfonso the Wise of Castile the suspicion that Jews kill Christian children, though not stated as fact, is at least admitted as a possibility. The relevant passage reads: "*Et porque oyemos decir*, que en algunos lugares los judios ficieron e facen el dia del viernes santo remembranza de la pasion de nuestro

The last remark is also important. That the Jews belong to the king, and that this creates a bond of common interest between them, is something of which Ibn Verga is keenly aware. When Gonzalo Martínez de Oviedo counsels Alfonso XI to expel the Jews, "Don Gil" (Aegidius Albornoz), the Archbishop of Toledo, vehemently opposes the plan:

> He said to Gonzalo: "Have they indeed made you advisor to the king? You have counseled shame upon your house! For behold, the Jews are a treasury to the king, a good treasury, but you seek to destroy them, and you urge the king to do what his fathers did not. You are not an enemy of the Jews but of the king!"[97]

Of course, ultimately even Ibn Verga cannot completely ignore the fact that sometimes kings have themselves proceeded against the Jews on their own initiative. In the context of the *Shebet Yehudah*, however, these are seen as departures from the norm, and they are few in number. Needless to say, not one of these instances concerns the kings of Spain. Furthermore, in the cases he does cite, Ibn Verga characteristically exerts himself to find some mitigating circumstance, however farfetched it may be. For example, in an obscure reference to one of the Byzantine persecutions he relates how a decree of forced conversion came forth from the emperor, but that when he saw the steadfastness of the Jews he had pity on them. In order now to appease his subjects, he compromised by merely issuing some restrictive ordinances.[98] Describing one of the French expulsions of the fourteenth century Ibn Verga notes that it was perpetrated by a "very cruel king." Still, he cannot resist adding a further nuance. When someone intercedes for the Jews, the king replies "that the people have already risen against the Jews, and their expulsion is their remedy and benefit; and he is expelling them in order to save them from their enemies and those who rise against them."[99] Most refractory to rationaliza-

---

sennor Jesu Christo en manera de escarnio furtando los ninnos et poniendolos en la cruz, o faciendo imagines de cera et crucificandolas, quando los ninnos non pueden haber, mandamos que si fama fuere daqui adelante que en algunt lugar de nuestro sennorio tal cosa sea fecha, si se pudiere averiguar, que todos aquellos que se acertaren en aquel fecho que sean presos et recabdados et aduchos antel rey, et despues que el sopiere la verdad, debe los mandar matar muy aviltadamente, quanto quier que sean" (*Las siete partidas*, VII, xxiv, 2, in F. [Y.] Baer, *Die Juden im Christlichen Spanien*, II, Kastilien/Inquisitionsakten [Berlin, 1936], p. 45). The intent of this law in the *Partidas*, it should be added, is clearly to protect the accused Jews from the lynch-law of the mob by insisting that all such cases be brought before the royal courts.

(97) *Shebet Yehudah*, Ch. 10, p. 54.
(98) *Shebet Yehudah*, Ch. 28, p. 72.
(99) *Shebet Yehudah*, Ch. 23, p. 69.

tion is the notorious forced conversion of Iberian Jewry by Sisebut in 613. Yet even here, Ibn Verga does not portray the Visigothic king as evil. At worst, he is presented as a religious zealot acting misguidedly for the exaltation of his faith. There is even a certain moral stature in his firm refusal to accept any bribe. To the Jews he declares: "I desire your welfare, so why do you reject it with both hands?"[100]

Because they violate the natural order, kings who deliberately harm the Jews are punished.[101] The Persian king who (unwillingly!) imposed a forced conversion subsequently "descended from one decline to another," until the Muslims came and conquered his realm.[102] The Almoravid chieftain Ibn Tumart allegedly converts the Jews and, as a result, dies within a month.[103] Philip IV of France, described as a "cruel king," expels the Jews in 1306.[104] But eventually he is thrown from his horse and killed, "and all knew that his cruelty toward the Jews caused him that death." Under his successor, Louis X, the Jews are recalled, the normal relationship is restored, and the king promises to guard them "as the apple of his eye."[105]

But what is *melekh ḥasid*, and how does a king come to merit such an encomium from Ibn Verga? We are helped by the fact that Manuel of Portugal is not the only monarch to whom this term, or variants thereof, is applied. The fictitious "Alfonso" is described as "the mighty and gracious king" (*ha-melekh ha-'adir vehe-ḥasid*).[106] Since the same Alfonso is called at other times "a just king" (*melekh mishpat*,[107] or *ha-melekh ha-yashar*[108]), the term *ḥasid* is presumably to be equated with these qualities. Thus Louis X of France is described as *melekh ḥesed ve-'oheb mishpat*, "a gracious king and lover of justice."[109] But there is more to this. Robert of Anjou is styled *melekh ḥesed ve-'oheb ha-yehudim*.[110] The two attributes somehow coalesce. To be a lover of justice is also to love the Jews and, consequently, to deal justly with them.

Still, such words as *ḥasid* or *ḥesed* ordinarily imply more than justice alone,

(100) *Shebet Yehudah*, Ch. 9, pp. 51 f.
(101) Though Usque does not at all share Ibn Verga's approach to kingship, the punishment of kings who maltreated the Jews is for him one of the great consolations which the Lord periodically affords His people (*Consolaçam*, III, 50 f.; ed. Cohen, 228 f.).
(102) *Shebet Yehudah*, Ch. 3, p. 21.
(103) *Ibid*., Ch. 4, pp. 21 f.
(104) *Ibid*., Ch. 21, p. 69.
(105) *Ibid*., Ch. 24, p. 70. See also Shohat's note, p. 187, *ad loc*.
(106) *Ibid*., Ch. 7, p. 26.
(107) *Ibid*., Ch. 8, p. 46.
(108) *Ibid*., Ch. 29, p. 72.
(109) *Ibid*., Ch. 24, p. 70.
(110) *Ibid*., Ch. 14, p. 61.

both in biblical and especially in postbiblical Hebrew. Indeed, they possess strong overtones of going considerably beyond the letter of the law.[111] While Robert of Anjou could merit such an appreciation from Jews,[112] it does seem rather extravagant when applied to Louis X. But of course it would be quite useless to indulge our modern sensibility and to protest that the latter's recall of French Jewry in 1315 betrays little more than mundane reasons of state. For Ibn Verga, Louis' action is sufficient to qualify him as *melekh ḥesed*, and it seems that at least in this particular case his opinion reflects that of others.[113] Were this all the *Shebet Yehudah* could offer on the subject, we should be content to say that Ibn Verga's use of *ḥesed* is merely based on what he views as the objective behavior of monarchs, without inquiring into their motives. Yet, probing further, we find that he is even quite prepared to extol some figures whose very acts were prejudicial to the Jews.

Thus Pope John XXII is called "a gracious man (*'ish ḥesed*), a speaker of righteousness, a speaker of rectitude, and, in his qualities and behavior, a man of truth."[114] This effusive description occurs in the context of a chapter (no. 14) recounting John's purported resistance to pressure from his sister for the expulsion of the Jews from the papal territories.[115] Nevertheless, the

(111) In this respect one should not lose sight of the one biblical verse in which *ḥesed* is applied to earthly kings. In I Kings 20:31, after Ben Hadad of Aram is defeated at the battle of Aphek and flees, his servants counsel him to surrender to Ahab of Israel, "for the kings of the house of Israel are gracious kings (מלכי חסד)." Commenting on this verse, Abravanel observes aptly: "that is to say—they are accustomed to perform acts of grace *gratuitously* (חנם) with all men" (*Comm. to the Bk. of Kings, ad loc.*).

(112) Cf. the effusive praise of Robert by his Jewish contemporaries Kalonymos b. Kalonymos (cited by A. M. Habermann in his ed. of the latter's *'Eben boḥan* [Tel Aviv, 1953], 187, n. 38), and Shemariah of Negroponte (Graetz, *Geschichte*, VII, 277, n. 2).

(113) This is indicated by Profiat Duran's similar reference to Louis as *melekh ḥasid* (in Abravanel, *Yeshu'ot meshiḥo*, 46r.), and by Usque's calling him "the virtuous Catholic King Louis" (*Consolaçam*, III, 22r.; ed. Cohen, 193). Nevertheless, the fact that Ibn Verga shares this appraisal of Louis with others in no way lessens its significance for an understanding of his own mentality. Even if he is quoting the phrase, he is thereby tacitly endorsing it. Though Joseph Ha-Kohen depends on Usque or on a common source for this account of the recall of the Jews to France, he says nothing whatever in praise of the king. See *'Emek ha-bakha*, 71.

(114) *Shebet Yehudah*, p. 60.

(115) Along with the parallel account in Usque (see next note) this marks the only reference to an attempted papal expulsion of Jews prior to the Counter-Reformation. On the questionable historicity of the events as described here, see Salo W. Baron, *A Social and Religious History of the Jews*, 2nd rev. ed. (New York, 1952 et seq.), X, 253 f., XI, 251 f., and the literature surveyed in the pertinent notes. Needless to say, we are here concerned, not with the accuracy of the facts, but with Ibn Verga's perception of those he had at his disposal.

use of such hyperboles remains odd, and it is hard to reconcile them with the account itself. Granted that the pope is initially depicted as arguing with his sister against the expulsion. But then Ibn Verga goes on to relate that he succumbed under further pressure, that the Jews had to engage in elaborate lobbying and bribery, that they succeeded in persuading Robert of Anjou to intercede on their behalf, and that even then the pope insisted on keeping his promise to his sister unless she change her mind. This was finally accomplished by a further bribe to her of one thousand florins, and only then was the edict rescinded. Taken on its own terms the story would seem to show, at best, that John was well meaning but ineffectual. Such, obviously, was not Ibn Verga's assessment. The pope who, if the account were historically reliable, came so perilously close to a radical break with the Jewish policy of all his predecessors is styled *'ish ḥesed*, and this even though the favorable outcome of the episode was independent of his efforts.[116]

To dispel any lingering doubts as to Ibn Verga's ability to salvage even the reputation of an overtly hostile ruler, we have but to turn to his treatment of Charles IV of France, who expelled the Jews in 1322. Describing that expulsion in Ch. 25, he writes: "But that king was an upright king (*melekh yashar*)." Why? Because "he expelled them with their goods and their money."[117] The seemingly fine qualification is not accidental, for in an

---

(116) In Ch. 6, it is true, Ibn Verga mentions the papal bull condemning the excesses against the Jews during the Shepherd Massacre (*Shebet Yehudah*, p. 23), and we must entertain the possibility that it was his pro-Jewish intervention which earned the pope the praises recorded in Ch. 14. However, since John is not actually named in either passage (he is merely called "the pope"), and no date is suggested for the abortive expulsion, there is no compelling reason to suppose that Ibn Verga even realized he was writing in both chapters about the same pope. To assume otherwise would raise the further question as to whether he did not also know that it was John who ordered the burning of the Talmud in 1320 (see my study of "The Papal Inquisition and the Jews of France in the Time of Bernard Gui," *Harvard Theological Review*, LXIII [1970], 327). The phrase *'ish ḥasid* occurs, significantly, not in Ch. 6, where at least it would have been more appropriate (Philip V of France is there called *melekh ḥasid*), but in Ch. 14, which should be viewed independently.

This chapter must finally be compared to the parallel account in Usque (*Consolaçam*, III, 19v; ed. Cohen, 190). Since both writers commit the same gross error in calling the pope's sister "Sancha," when this was actually the name of the wife of Robert of Anjou, it is obvious that Ibn Verga and Usque depend, whether directly or ultimately, on a common source. Hence the difference between the two is all the more glaring. In the *Consolaçam* there is not a hint of praise for the pope, and we may well presume there was none in the source. The argumentative dialogues between the pope and his sister in the *Shebet Yehudah* are so reflective of the author's style throughout the book, the exaggerated praise so consistent with his basic attitude, that we can only regard them as Ibn Verga's purposeful embellishments.

(117) *Shebet Yehudah*, Ch. 25, p. 70.

44

earlier chapter he has emphasized the converse. If Charles IV was "upright" because he allowed the banished Jews to take their assets with them, Philip IV was "cruel," because in the expulsion of 1306 "he took all they had, their silver and gold, their movables and their land, and they were expelled in nakedness and lacking everything."[118]

Now if this distinction can serve Ibn Verga as a dividing line between "justice" and "cruelty," then not only is his entire notion of royal justice placed in a new light but, by extension, his use of *ḥasid* as well. In effect, we must ignore some of the ordinary resonances which such a word retains and savor it afresh within the framework of Ibn Verga's consistent exaltation of royalty. So gripped is he by the idea of royal benevolence to the Jews in general that, paradoxically, he can have a remarkably low threshold of expectation in concrete instances. What is required in order for a Charles IV to be called just by Ibn Verga we have observed.[119] Any positive act of a king

(118) *Ibid.*, Ch. 21. By calling attention to Ibn Verga's use of *melekh yashar* in the context of the expulsion by Charles IV, I by no means propose to minimize the seriousness of the confiscation issue for the exiles themselves. Quite the contrary, once an edict of expulsion was promulgated this issue obviously became crucial. Ibn Verga was thus not alone in underscoring the difference in this regard between the French expulsions of 1306 and 1322. We find it in Duran (Abravanel, *Yeshu'ot Meshiḥo*, 46r), in Usque (*Consolaçam*, III, 22r; ed. Cohen, 193), and in Joseph Ha-Kohen ('*Emek ha-bakha*, 71), all again pointing to a common source. These three works also note that the expulsion of 1322 came, not on the king's initiative, but as a result of the demand of "the people." In view of these common features, however, it remains significant that only Ibn Verga actually employs the phrase *melekh yashar*, the other writers being content merely to record that no confiscation took place, without further comment.

(119) By the sixteenth century, as the experience of Jewish expulsion became ever more frequent, the attitude expressed by Ibn Verga became all the more widespread. Describing the situation in Italy around the mid-sixteenth century Isaiah Sonne made the telling observation that "the expulsion of Jews from one state to another was then a normal phenomenon, and the expelled did not regard it as a work of evil. They knew very well that their stay was temporary and the time fixed by contract, and that when the time expired they must be prepared to vacate the place and seek a new home. They were well aware that the ruler had the right to cancel the contract before it expired. Consequently, the fact of expulsion was insufficient of itself to stamp the banisher as a persecutor of Jews. The touchstone was the *mode* of expulsion. If the other side fulfilled all the clauses of the agreement designed to protect the person and property of the Jews, and made no attempt to confiscate their money and send them forth emptyhanded, the rulers were then considered righteous kings whom one could serve faithfully even after the expulsion" (*Mi-Pavlo ha-rebi'i 'ad Pius ha-ḥamishi* [Jerusalem, 1954], 140 f.). We must recognize, however, that what was "natural" to Jews in the Italy of the *condotta*, or to Ashkenazic Jews even earlier, was less so to a Sephardic Jew who, like Ibn Verga, had grown to maturity in pre-Expulsion Spain. There, theory notwithstanding, Jewish residence had not been *felt* as a mere matter of temporary contractual sufferance. That many among the upper echelons of Spanish

toward the Jews is occasion for praise. Moreover, royal actions are apparently quite separable, and the good can be lauded independently of the adverse. Convinced, as were most of his class, that kings are fundamentally committed to the rule of law and the preservation of their Jews, he is always prepared to give them the benefit of the doubt. Where kings appear sometimes to violate the established pattern Ibn Verga will extend himself, as we have seen, to find some mitigating factor that may explain the aberration or soften its implications.

If, on the whole, the royal alliance has operated in favor of the Jews in other countries, how much more so in Spain itself. Trouble for the Jews may certainly loom from any quarter, for they have many enemies. But Jewish courtiers in the *Shebet Yehudah* move with ease and confidence through the castles of the kings of Castile and Aragon. They have the ear of the kings and, so long as these have the power, royal justice triumphs in the end. Of the many examples in the book, it will suffice to cite one of the most notable. The chapter concerns yet another blood-libel against the Jews, though both the story and dialogue are patently fictional. A corpse is discovered in the house of a Spanish Jew. One of the king's advisors supports the charge of ritual murder, and the people clamor for vengeance. But the king will have none of this:

> Then he summoned all the Jews before him, and when they came, he asked: "What did David mean when he said (Ps. 121:4)—*Behold, the Guardian of Israel doth neither slumber nor sleep*, since if He does not slumber then surely He does not sleep! For I have heard that in the Hebrew tongue sleep is more than slumber."
>
> The Jews replied: "That which the commentators have explained to us is simply that He does not slumber, and therefore He certainly does not sleep."
>
> The king said: "That is to answer the question with the question itself. They have not understood the intent of the verse, but here is its explanation, as I see it. Last night I could not in any way rest or sleep. So I rose from by bed, went to the outer court, and put my head out of the window. The moon was shining, and I saw men running, one of

---

Jewry were pervaded by a general feeling of security even in the final decade before the Expulsion is perhaps most eloquently attested by Isaac Abravanel. See his introductions to *Ma'ayeney ha-yeshu'ah* (Stettin, 1860, fol. 2v–3r), *Zebaḥ Pesaḥ* (Constantinople, 1505, 2r), and to his *Commentary on Deuteronomy*. Thus, although Ibn Verga's attitude toward Charles IV and other royal figures may at first seem identical with that described by Sonne for a subsequent generation elsewhere, I believe its roots to be quite different. His own extreme faith in monarchs would seem by far the dominant factor.

whom carried on his back what seemed like a human body. I sent three men to follow them slowly and to tell me if the man had been killed, or what was the matter. My servants went as I had commanded and, placing themselves in ambush, saw that he was slain. They recognized two of the men who were leading the corpse away, and these witnesses stand before you."

The witnesses came and testified, and the king's advisor asked: "Why did you not apprehend them?" They replied that [the culprits] hurried, threw the corpse into the courtyard of the Jew and then fled. "Moreover, they were armed and we had nothing in hand, for the king did not command us to capture them, only to see what was the matter."

Thereupon the king returned to his theme and declared: "This is why the verse states *Behold He neither slumbers nor sleeps*, that is to say—He does not slumber, nor does He allow him who is the guardian of Israel to sleep."

Then they all departed with fear in their souls, and upon the slanderers he wreaked vengeance.[120]

In this singular exegesis Ibn Verga has transferred the biblical epithet "Guardian of Israel" (*shomer Yisrael*) from God to the king of Spain. The exaltation of the king, at least in relation to the Jews, borders here on apotheosis.[121]

(120) *Shebet Yehudah*, Ch. 16, pp. 62 f.

(121) Ibn Verga's story itself probably derives from another source. A. Shohat (p. 184, *ad loc.*) has pointed out the closely parallel tale, set in Constantinople, which appears in the *Ma'aseh Book* (see M. Gaster's ed. [Philadelphia, 1934], II, no. 185, pp. 400 f.). There, however, the phrase "Guardian of Israel" is still applied exclusively to God, as in the biblical context. Although, in the absence of Ibn Verga's immediate source, we cannot be certain, it seems likely that the shift of *Shomer Yisrael* from God to the king represents his own exegetical twist.

A somewhat similar shift of another famous biblical phrase intimately associated with God takes place in Ch. 29, p. 72, where the verse "Shall not the judge of all the earth do justice" (Gen. 18:25) is referred to "Alfonso" king of Spain. Here, to be sure, it is used in an ironic context, a Christian mob demanding that the king punish a Jew for ritual murder. On the other hand, cf. Isaac Abravanel's autobiographical description of his flight to Castile from charges of conspiracy in Portugal (Int. to *Comm. on the Former Prophets*), stating that he wrote to the Portuguese king in these terms: "Save, O king! Is it good that thou shouldst oppress? *Shall not the judge of all the earth do justice?*!" Abraham's challenge to the Lord is here addressed to João II of Portugal. While it would be absurd to take this transference literally, and while it is undoubtedly not as conscious as Ibn Verga's manipulation of *Shomer Yisrael*, the psychic process which enables a Jew to speak of a gentile king in words so closely linked to God is not without relevance to our theme.

In the same sense we should take cognizance of the equally striking application of Ps. 85:8 ("Show us Thy mercy, O Lord, and grant us Thy salvation") to Pope Benedict

But if the kings of Spain were the guardians of the Jews then why, in the final analysis, were the latter expelled in 1492? This is, after all, the central problem in the *Shebet Yehudah*, and whatever the other ambiguities in the book, it would seem that in two key passages Ibn Verga's answer is quite explicit. In Chapter 24, while discussing the recall of the Jews to France in 1315, he writes:

For generally the kings of Spain and France, the nobles and savants, and all the distinguished persons of the land, used to love the Jews, and hatred fell only among the populace, who were jealous of the Jews.

[While some of the French exiles said]: But if the king makes promises to us and then the people rise, how can we be secure, especially since we have seen that in the past the people brought several expulsions upon us? What gain is there in the benevolence of the king [*ḥesed ha-melekh*] and the judges of the land, if the will of the peoples is not with us and they constantly seek our ruin? Therefore let us remain where we are and not bring upon ourselves the wrath of expulsions, and never experience them again.

But after a short while they changed their minds and said: Come, let us return to the land of our birth for it is our mother, and the king is good and upright. What he has spoken he will fulfill.[122]

Again, in Chapter 44, the Jews of Spain are threatened with expulsion unless they convert:

XIII in *Shebet Yehudah* Ch. 40, describing the Disputation of Tortosa. One of the Jewish delegates, Samuel Halevi, cries out to the pope: "Show us thy mercy, our lord, and grant us thy salvation" (*ibid.*, p. 96, line 28). Here, to be sure, the Tetragrammaton in the verse is changed to אדונינו. Further on, however, (p. 99, lines 29 f.), God's name in the first part of the verse, though applied to the pope, is allowed to remain, while the second part is now referred to the assembled bishops. Thus: אמרו השלוחים: כבר הראנו אדונינו האפיפיור מה ששאלנו מאתו: "הראנו ה' חסדך", "ועליכם ההגמונים הקדושים אמר: "וישעך תתן לנו". The account by Bonastruc Desmaestre, on which Ibn Verga says he based himself, has apparently not survived. In the only other extant Hebrew report of the disputation the same verse from Psalms is also addressed to the pope, but its impact is softened by an immediate explanation that it is really God who will move him to act mercifully toward the Jews: ואמר "הראנו נא חסדך וישעך תתן לנו," ויסד דבריו כי אנחנו בטוחים בשם ית' שישים בלב האפיפיור שיעשה עמנו חסדים וטובות (S. Halberstam, "Vikuaḥ Tortosa," in Kobak's *Jeschurun*, VI [1868], Hebrew section, 48). This explanation, and the deletion of the name of God from the verse itself, indicates that the writer, unlike Ibn Verga, was at least sensitive to the incongruity of transferring such a verse to the pope in the first place. See the recent study and translation (into Catalan) of both Hebrew texts by Jaume Riera i Sans, *La crònica en Hebreu de la Disputa de Tortosa* (Barcelona, 1974), especially p. 41, n. 35.
    (122) *Shebet Yehudah*, p. 70.

And when the Jews heard this they went to one of the king's ministers, for he loved them greatly, as in Spain they were beloved of the kings, the nobles, and all their wise men and savants, and were much honored by them. The expulsions emanated only because of some of the lower classes who claimed that because of the Jews and their arrival in the kingdom their own food became expensive, and that the Jews also encroached upon their trades. The expulsions also derived from the priests, for in a display of piety, and in order to show the people that they seek to honor and exalt the religion of Jesus the Nazarene, they would daily preach bitter things against the Jews. But by the other Christian classes the Jews were honored as though they lived in their own land, and they were much loved by them, as is known to the elders of Spain.[123]

The thrust of these passages is evident. Throughout the *Shebet Yehudah* Ibn Verga shows himself well aware that the Jews everywhere face a constellation of different forces. On the one hand—kings (along with the aristocracy) and the papacy; on the other—the masses and the lower clergy. The former are generally well disposed to the Jews; the latter, usually hostile. The kings and the masses especially are in tension concerning the Jews. Kings represent a constant, but the masses are fickle. Though ever ready to protect the Jews, the kings are sometimes prevented from doing so by their own subjects.

Ibn Verga never budges from this basic position. Not once do we hear in the *Shebet Yehudah*, whether directly or by implication, that the expulsion of Spanish Jewry in 1492 was due to a fundamental change in attitude on the part of the Crown. Like so many of his generation and his class, Ibn Verga was obviously jolted by the catastrophe. He had, perforce, to re-examine the archetypal relationship between king and Jews and ask himself if it had not suffered some radical dislocation. As may be seen in the passages just quoted, and is evident in numerous historical anecdotes which, though set elsewhere, contain obvious references to the Spanish situation, Ibn Verga's answer is negative. The change occurred, not in the basic attitude of the Crown, but in the growth of religious fanaticism and popular hostility, both welling up to such a pitch that they could no longer be resisted. In short, whatever else the *Shebet Yehudah* may be, it remains, even if indirectly, an absolution of the king of Spain from real culpability in the Expulsion. There is not a word nor a hint that the royal alliance itself had reached an impasse, that for various reasons the Crown now felt it no longer really needed the Jews and would gain from their elimination.

But in late fifteenth-century Spain the Crown was, after all, a dual one.

(123) *Ibid.*, pp. 117 f.

Ferdinand and Isabella ruled in a personal union of Aragon and Castile, and the Edict of Expulsion is signed *Yo el Rey, Yo la Reina*. Though neither is ever mentioned by name in the *Shebet Yehudah*, Ibn Verga leaves little doubt as to which of the two is the culprit. It was the bigoted queen, herself a tool of the clergy. In Chapter 44, from which we quoted above, the reference to Isabella and her former confessor, Torquemada, is transparent:

> In Spain there was a priest who greatly hated the Jews . . . and he was confessor to the queen. He incited the queen to force the Jews to convert, and if not, that they perish by the sword. And the queen pleaded with the king and begged this of him. After several days the king accepted his wife's advice that they convert, but if not—that they all go forth and be expelled from his kingdom. And the documents were written and signed at the king's command.[124]

Ibn Verga is undeterred by facts of which, as a contemporary, he was surely cognizant. The nature of the dual monarchy of the Catholic Kings is here completely ignored in order to fit them into the archetype. The king holds the reins of power alone. The queen is merely the nagging wife, and not, as Isabella actually was in Castile, a sovereign in her own right. Moreover, even if the project for expulsion had first been broached by Isabella, there is no evidence whatever that Ferdinand did not accept it with equal enthusiasm. The policy, like so many others, was a joint one. But Ibn Verga's attitude to the royal couple is confirmed in a blatantly fictional ending to the chapter. After the Jews have offered a bribe of fifty thousand gold pieces we are told:

> That same night the servants of the king testified that they saw the priest speak lustfully to the queen. They summoned the queen, and she admitted it. The king commanded that [the priest] be hanged on a tree. Then at his command the documents [of the Expulsion] were brought and torn up, for the king knew that [the priest] had incited the queen to request it, *and the king had acquiesced against his will*, and the money was returned to the Jews.[125]

However, there is also an important corollary to Ibn Verga's central thesis. Granted that kings are a favorable constant and the masses at best unpredictable. But if the latter can often vitiate the good-will of the sovereign, then

---

(124) *Ibid.*, p. 117. That this chapter really has Ferdinand and Isabella in its background is evident, not only in the reference to the queen's confessor [קונפיסור], but by the mention of the converso Martín de Lucena, a contemporary of the author denounced to the Inquisition in 1481.

(125) *Ibid.*, p. 118. Characteristically, Ibn Verga concludes the chapter on an equivocal note: "And there is another, oral version of this, but this is what I found written."

for their own self-preservation the Jews must do all they possibly can to neutralize the masses in relation to themselves. For this the intervention of Jewish courtiers with the king is not enough. Jews at large must so conduct themselves in their daily lives as to reduce potential frictions with the rest of the population. They should, on the whole, display a low profile, avoid ostentation in dress, and refrain from flaunting their luxuries in any way. Those Jews who, as tax farmers or in other positions, wield power over Christians should be wary of excess. Though popular hatred can perhaps not be eradicated, it need not be stupidly inflamed. Yet this is precisely what the Jews have done, especially in Spain. Running as a leitmotif through the *Shebet Yehudah* is the notion that often the Jews themselves are to blame for their own misfortunes.[126] On this score, ironically, Ibn Verga is at one with the most pietistic moralists of the generation of the Spanish exiles.[127] Both, in essence, dwell on the sins of the Jews themselves as a cause for the Expulsion. Both castigate the *hubris* of their coreligionists and even list many of the same particulars. But whereas for the preachers these constitute religious sins which have brought down the wrath of God, Ibn Verga apprehends them as essentially profane errors which have elicited the ire of the masses. In this, as in other aspects, both his originality and his limitations stand revealed. Alone among his generation (at least of those who have recorded their thoughts in writing) Ibn Verga ventured to analyze Jewish historical suffering in terms of what he himself calls "natural cause" (*ha-sibbah ha-ṭibʿit*), and not merely

(126) So, for example, the words uttered, as it were, by "Tomás" in Ch. 7, p. 30: "There is no remedy for hatred which derives from envy. . . . When the Jews first settled in the kingdom of our lord they would come like slaves and exiles, dressed in tattered rags, and for many years they did not wear fine clothes nor display any arrogance, and in those days did you ever hear, my lord, that they were accused of eating blood? . . . But now the Jew plays the aristocrat, and if he has two hundred gold *sueldos* he forthwith decks himself out in silk, and his sons in embroidery, which even princes with an annual income of a thousand *doblas* do not do. Therefore they are slandered, in the hope that this will result in their expulsion."

(127) It should be pointed out, however, that one major theme of the moralists—the notion that the Expulsion was linked to the excessive devotion of Spanish Jews to philosophy and other "alien" sciences—is entirely absent in the *Shebet Yehudah*. The point would not be noteworthy were it not for the text recently discovered by M. Benayahu (*supra*, n. 9). Here we learn that, prior to leaving Portugal, Ibn Verga apparently risked his life together with three kabbalists to salvage and smuggle out of the country a unique manuscript of Shemtob Ibn Shemtob's violently anti-philosophical work, *Sefer ha-'emunot*. Nothing in the *Shebet Yehudah*, nor the few facts hitherto available about its author, would have prepared us to place Ibn Verga in the anti-rationalists' camp. If the report in Benayahu's published text be true, it must necessarily provoke a re-examination of some aspects of the *Shebet Yehudah* itself, a task which cannot be undertaken here.

in terms of traditional theodicies. But while that step deserves, and has received, due recognition on the part of modern scholars, his much-vaunted originality should not be exaggerated either. The broader dynamics of the Expulsion are hardly perceived by him. Its relation to the final completion of the *Reconquista* by the Catholic Kings, to their general drive for national unity, to the Inquisition and the Converso problem, are beyond the ken of the book. The actions and motives of the Crown are not re-examined. Ibn Verga remained in the grip of inherited conceptions which even the stress of the Expulsion could not loosen.

Much has been written concerning the reaction of Spanish Jewry to the trauma of their expulsion, but almost nothing about their specific attitudes toward those who expelled them. A careful survey will reveal that Ibn Verga's tacit absolution of the Crown was, even when stemming from different premises, far from unusual or eccentric.

Throughout the literature of the Spanish exiles it is God's justice which looms as problematic, rather than that of the Spanish state. As was always the case with expulsions in other countries,[128] so here, too, no one, whether Jew or Christian, seems to have questioned the intrinsic *right* of the Catholic Kings to expel the Jews. After all, the ultimate authority of the king over the privilege of Jewish residence, deriving from his basic ownership of the land, had long been regarded as axiomatic.[129] On a theoretical level, Jews themselves would not have disputed the formulation of the Portuguese Diogo Lopes Rebelo in a political treatise on kingship written for Dom Manuel some four years after the expulsion from Spain. "The king," he states tersely, "can in good conscience, and without any sin whatever, retain the Jews in the kingdom; similarly, in good conscience, and without any sin whatever, he can expel them from his kingdom."[130]

(128) See Salo W. Baron, *The Jewish Community* (Philadelphia, 1942), I, 215 f.

(129) E.g., Rabbi Solomon b. Adret: "Precisely in the case of gentile kings did they say 'the law of the kingdom is law' (*dina de-malkhuta dina*) . . . because the king can say to them—'If you will not obey my commands, I will exile you,' for the land belongs to him" (*Novellae* to *Nedarim*, 28a, citing the Tosafot ascribed to R. Eliezer of Metz; the same statement is also cited by R. Nissim of Gerona, Comm. to *Nedarim, ad loc.*). For other sources, and a discussion of the extent and limits of royal power recognized by Spanish halakhists, see Shalom Albeck, "Dina de-malkhuta dina bi-kehilot Sefarad" ["The Law of the Kingdom is Law" in the Jewish Communities of Spain], *Abraham Weiss Jubilee Volume* (New York, 1964), Hebrew Section, 109–25; cf. Neuman, *Jews in Spain*, I, 7 ff. In the light of the aforementioned formulation, see also *Shebet Yehudah*, Ch. 4, p. 22, where Ibn Verga has the Jews say to the Almoravid Ibn Tumart: "Thou art our king, and we thy people, and if we do not do thy will, then thou shalt exile us to another land . . ."

(130) *Do governo da república pelo Rei* (*De Republica Gubernanda per Regem*), facsimile of ed. 1496, edited with a Portuguese translation by Artur Moreira de Sá (Lisbon, 1951),

But in this instance Jews accepted more than theory. Haim Hillel Ben-Sasson has shown to what a startling degree the Spanish religio-political rationale for the Expulsion was internalized in certain Jewish circles of the time. If Ibn Verga assimilated and reflects some of the popular charges against the Jews long current in Spain, others went far beyond him in their perception of the consolidating thrust of the Spanish monarchy in the late fifteenth century, and in their acceptance of its consequences. In their view, it was only natural that the drive toward Spanish national and political unification should be accompanied by an equal desire for religious homogeneity. Indeed, they could not gainsay that the Spanish Christian state was using correct means for the attainment of its objectives. Only the final goal was incorrect, and this merely because the Christian religion was itself false. However, if a Jewish king were to use the very same means, he would be absolutely justified. In retrospect, the age-old tolerant policy of the kings of Spain seemed now to have been a "miracle."[131]

On whatever level the generation of the Expulsion attempted to explain the catastrophe, the blame tended to gravitate away from the monarchy itself. Whether, as in the *Shebet Yehudah*, expulsion came because of the irresistible force of clerical and popular hatred (the latter partly provoked by the Jews) or, as the moralists had it, because the Lord had chastised His people for their transgressions, or, finally, because of the imminent consequences implicit in Spanish unification, the Crown stood somehow exonerated of any real guilt in the matter. To that extent, as well, the traditional royal archetype, though shaken, was not shattered.

Nowhere can this be seen so clearly as in the separate treatment accorded the figures of Ferdinand and Isabella in the Jewish literature of the age. Fortuitously, the very existence of the dual monarchy made such a separation possible in Jewish minds.

With virtual unanimity the Jewish writers clearly differentiate between the king and the queen, and heap almost all the blame upon the latter. It was Isabella who goaded Ferdinand into taking the step and persuaded him to

---

Ch. XII ("In quo tractatur de legibus et de earum condicionibus quas rex suis subditis de suo regno debet imponere"), pp. 134, 136: "Quid de judaeis qui parvae utilitati sunt in regno et blasphemant nomen Domini Jesu Christi, et utuntur in suis negotiis quadam caliditatis astutia? Utrum jure forent a regno expellendi? Respondetur quod rex cum bona conscientia, sine ullo peccato, potest eos tenere in regno; similiter cum bona conscientia et sine peccato potest eos expellere a regno suo. Ideo istud regis arbitrio reliquantur, et faciat rex bene consultus quid magis expediens sit regno suo." On the author and his work, see Francisco Elias de Tejada, "Diogo Lopes Rebelo, nuestro mas antiguo tratadista en derecho político," *Revista de estudios políticos*, XIV (1946), 163–79.

(131) H. H. Ben-Sasson, "Dor goley Sefarad 'al 'aẓmo," especially pp. 53–59.

53

overcome whatever scruples he may have had. "And the Lord waxed angry against His people and expelled it from the land of Castile through the king Don Herando [*sic*] and the advice of *his accursed wife, the wicked Isabella . . .*"[132] "For the enemies of my good fortune found the king *and much more so the queen*, Isabel, inclined to persecute me."[133] "And it is known that in the year [5]235 [i.e., 1475], there ruled in Spain the wicked Isabella, *and it is she who committed all these great evils.*"[134] It is as though to the degree that Isabella serves to siphon off Jewish indignation, Ferdinand emerges relatively unscathed. One is hard put to find the king's name accompanied by invectives comparable to those lavished on the queen. The worst occurs in a single statement by Isaac Abravanel, where Ferdinand is called "Asmodai, chief of all the demons."[135] On another occasion Abravanel calls him "Esau," but it is clear from the context that the label connotes nothing more than the king's religious zeal, awakened by his conquest of Granada. More interesting psychologically is the well-known description that follows of Abravanel's unsuccessful personal intercession with the king, while "the queen stood at his side to goad him on, and inclined him with her profuse talk to accomplish his deed from beginning to end."[136]

(132) Abraham b. Solomon Ardutiel, in: Neubauer, *Medieval Jewish Chronicles*, I, 111.

(133) Usque, *Consolaçam*, III, 25v; ed. Cohen, 198.

(134) Abraham b. Eliezer Halevi, cited by G. Scholem, *Kirjath Sefer*, II, 137.

(135) Abravanel, *Mirkebet ha-Mishnah* (ed. princeps of his Commentary on Deuteronomy, Sabbioneta, 1551), fol. 2a: העיר ה' רוח אשמדי ראש המחבלים מלך עריץ המולך במלכיות ספרד מרוב אונים וחסן הוא כאלונים לגרש את כל היהודים מכל מחווי ארצו גדולים וקטנים. This passage was printed but censored out in ink from most extant copies of the Sabbioneta edition, and is entirely absent in all subsequent editions down to our own day. See S. Z. Leiman's valuable study of "Abarbanel and the Censor," *Journal of Jewish Studies*, XIX (1968), 49–61. (I wish to thank my student Bezalel Safran for drawing this information to my attention).

Though we cannot be entirely certain, there is every likelihood that the passage is authentic, and not an interpolation of the Sabbioneta printers. If so, Leiman observes correctly that in light of it the common assumption that Abravanel harbored no personal animosity must be revised. Indeed, it is possible that similar expressions of hostility to Ferdinand in other works by Abravanel have been lost as a result of censorship or self-censorship. In the total absence of original or contemporary manuscripts of Abravanel, this question cannot be resolved. However, such speculations cannot alter the pattern that emerges from the writings of Abraham b. Solomon Ardutiel, Abraham b. Eliezer Halevi, Elijah Capsali and others, whose works remained in manuscript until modern times, and were thus never subjected to censorship. As for Abravanel himself, the vital issue concerns, not the degree of his subsequent hostility toward Ferdinand, but his clear implication that in the end it was Isabella who wrecked his intervention with the king and thus sealed the doom of Spanish Jewry.

(136) Abravanel, *Comm. on the Bk. of Kings*, Introduction. The entire account of the Spanish expulsion contained therein was interpolated into the Shebet Yehudah as Ch. 51

By the time the reports of the Expulsion reached the ears of a man like Rabbi Elijah Capsali in Crete, they had assumed full-blown legendary proportions. The account given in his *Seder Eliyahu Zuta* is undoubtedly woven out of anecdotes he had heard in his youth from the Sephardic exiles who arrived on the island and deserves to be quoted at length. After a discussion of the purported Jewish lineage of Ferdinand of Aragon and of the critical role played by Abraham Senior and other Jews in arranging his marriage to Isabella, Capsali observes that "the queen, Isabella, dominated him and inclined him to whatsoever she wished, swaying him with her glib mouth."[137] During the conquest of Granada,

> the wicked queen Isabel was our nemesis. Since the time of her marriage she quarreled daily with her husband [saying] "send forth the Jews from before me and let them depart!" For the priests had moved her heart and she had turned into an enemy of Israel. . . . And when she saw that the king did not heed her, she said to him: "You have reason to love the Jews, for you are bone of their bone and flesh of their flesh, and that is why the Jews married me off to you, so that you may be a support and a crutch to them." The king heard this evil thing and it greatly angered him. He removed the shoe from his foot, threw it at the queen's head, and struck her. The queen fled from him, and the hatred waxed between them for many days. But when the king waged his war [against Granada], he recalled what Isabel had said to him, and he thought: "I shall fulfill the wish of the queen lest she taunt me that I am of the seed of the Jews." Also because by virtue of this his god will hear him, when he brings to his religion a people too numerous to count. And so both sovereigns [set themselves] to do evil to the Jews.[138]

Following his description of the promulgation of the edict and the unsuccessful audience in which Abravanel and Senior both appeared before the sovereigns, Capsali continues:

> At that time both the aforementioned sages took counsel together to write their words very explicitly in an epistle and to send it to Isabel

by the editor, Joseph Ibn Verga. Abravanel's negotiations with Ferdinand and Isabella to avert the expulsion are analyzed in detail by Benzion Netanyahu, *Don Isaac Abravanel: Statesman and Philosopher* (Philadelphia, 1953), 53–58. He argues persuasively that Ferdinand was the prime mover throughout, "while Isabella was undoubtedly in favor of the expulsion, but was not the moving spirit behind it." His assertion that "if Abravanel placed major responsibility upon her, it was both because he misjudged Ferdinand and because Isabella was more open-minded and impulsive" (*ibid.*, 56) does not, in my opinion, probe deeply enough.

(137) Capsali, *Likkutim*, ed. Lattes, 63.
(138) *Ibid.*, 66 f.

the queen so that she may see them, thinking—"perhaps by this the wicked woman will yield to us and we shall live and not die." So the sage Don Isaac Abravanel wrote a letter to Isabel the queen, and he spoke to her harshly, paying no homage to the Crown. . . . He wrote that the Lord, be He blessed, will wreak the vengeance of the Jews upon her and her house and much more in that vein. He reminded her of all those who had done evil unto Israel, and they perished in the end. Also Don Abraham Senior wrote to her . . .

When the letters were given to the queen . . . she shuddered greatly at the words of Don Isaac Abravanel, for his hand had fallen heavily upon her, and his mouth was full of chastisement. She sought to have him captured, but he fled . . .[139]

Yet, of the writers of the time, it is Abravanel himself who at one point reveals his awareness of the full complicity of both king and queen in the expulsion. In another work he writes:

And the Lord raised as an adversary against its [i.e. Spanish Jewry's] peace and tranquility, Don Ferando [sic], a great king over a vast realm, there is no end to his greatness, ruling throughout the kingdom of Spain and Sicily and their islands, and in all the places of his dominion he affects the greatest piety in his faith, clinging to his law and his religion. *Kings of hosts they were, two of them, husband and wife, who together brazened their heart to humble the pride of Judah* . . .[140]

If, nonetheless, the prevailing image of the Catholic Kings among the Spanish exiles was one which made Isabella the villainess, while Ferdinand emerged a comparatively passive character in the drama, it was because such an interpretation fitted the archetypes epitomized in Ibn Verga's book. Though the tragedy of the expulsion was of unprecedented magnitude, such an analysis of the royal couple could be subsumed to recognizable patterns. The king influenced by his vicious wife—it was, after all, a repetition of other such instances of woman's wiles, of the Jew-hating sister of Pope John XXII who pressed him to expel the Jews,[141] or the queen of "France" who begged the king to do the same, "and he did not want to do it, for the Jews were important in his eyes . . . and he tried daily to deter the queen . . . but finally

(139) *Ibid.*, 70–72.

(140) Abravanel, Int. to *Ma'ayeney ha-yeshu'ah*. Cf. also the anonymous contemporary account, probably of Italian provenance but very well informed on events, published by A. Marx (*JQR*, XX, 249 ff.) where Ferdinand is the main actor throughout. Even here, however, not a harsh word is said about him.

(141) *Shebet Yehudah*, no. 14, p. 60.

gave in to her wishes."[142] In its dominant form the Ferdinand-Isabella image does not impair the royal archetype, for it is itself archetypal. And let us not ignore the specific echoes of the name "Isabella" to Jewish ears, recalling, as it does, the biblical Jezebel of the Book of Kings who had also spurred her royal spouse to commit atrocities.

Of course, no criticism of Spanish Jewry is necessarily implied in bringing these attitudes to the Catholic Kings into relief, for they are but further consequences of the Hispano-Jewish historical experience. Seen in that light, the very efforts of Spanish Jewry on behalf of Ferdinand and Isabella prior to the Expulsion must have seemed realistic at the time, for a traditional identity of interest indicated that the union of Aragon and Castile and the strengthening of the Crown would prove a boon to the Jews. If the Edict of Expulsion came as an unexpected shock, it was not because they did not know that the Crown had the right to expel them, but because it simply did not occur to them that the right would be exercised. Even when the deed was done it was supremely difficult, for most perhaps impossible, to abandon the royal myth altogether, for that would have meant an admission that the entire direction in which the courtier class had guided the destinies of Spanish Jewry had been based on false premises. And so, with regard to the Crown itself, Isabella-Jezebel absorbed most of the blame and the rancor.

Again, as we have stressed, any of the theodicies current in the age of the Expulsion tended intrinsically to deflect responsibility from the Crown, or to render it somehow irrelevant. It all depended on the perspective. Thus, on another occasion Abravanel comes to speak of the messianic implications of the European expulsions, arguing that the divine plan was thereby to shift the geographical locus of Jewry eastward, and hence closer to Palestine. It is somewhat unnerving to discover that in this passage Abravanel applies to the European kings generally, and to Ferdinand and Isabella specifically, the biblical phrase associated with none other than Cyrus the Great when he restored the Jews to Palestine from their Babylonian exile:

Moreover, we have seen with our own eyes that the *Lord stirred up the spirit*[143] of the kings of the Western lands to expel from their domains

(142) *Ibid.*, no. 20, p. 67. Though France is mentioned here, the chapter clearly refers to England. See Shohat's note, p. 185, *ad loc.*

(143) The quotation is from Ezra 1:1 (= II Chron. 36:22): העיר ה' את רוח כרש מלך פרס. Cf. Jer. 51:11, where the same phrase is used in connection with the vengeance to be wreaked upon Babylon through the Medes (העיר ה' את רוח מלכי מדי כי על בבל מזמתו). In a slightly different form, it is applied to Zerubbabel and his associates, who were stirred to rebuilt the Temple (Hag., 1:14), and to the king of Assyria who was stirred to exile the Northern tribes of Israel (I Chron. 5:26). In the latter instance, of course, there are no redemptive implications whatever.

57

all the Jews who lived there, the first exile beginning from the isle at the edge of the world called England. . . . And in the year [5]252 [i.e., 1492] *the Lord stirred up the spirit* of the kings of Spain to expel the Jews from their land, about three hundred thousand souls, in such a manner that they all emerged from all parts of the West, and all passed toward the Land of Israel . . .[144]

Be that as it may, it seemed as clear as ever that, until the Redemption would actually take place, essentially no other options existed in the post-Expulsion period than had obtained earlier in Spain. Abravanel and others of his class went forth in their exile to serve other kings in near and far-off places, and in the very attempt at the reconstruction of Jewish life in the Sephardic diaspora the royal alliance seemed once more to be pragmatically confirmed. Reporting his arrival in Naples, where he and other refugees found temporary shelter, Abravanel writes—"and I, amidst the exiled, came with all my household . . . here to the renowned city of Naples, *whose kings are gracious kings (malkhey ḥesed)* . . ."[145]

(144) Abravanel, *Comm. on the Latter Prophets*, ad Isa. 43:6. That the culminating European expulsion was divinely ordained as the prologue to redemption is a view shared by others, such as Abraham b. Eliezer Halevi and Elijah Capsali. But these writers more naturally identify the Ottoman Turkish sultans with Cyrus. (See Charles Berlin: "A 16th-Century Hebrew Chronicle of the Ottoman Empire: The *Seder Eliyahu Zuta* of Elijah Capsali and its Message," *Studies in Jewish Bibliography, History and Literature* [New York, 1971], 28 ff. and *passim*.) Similarly, several centuries earlier Judah Al-Ḥarizi had described Saladin as having been stirred by the Lord to conquer Jerusalem from the Crusaders in 1190: . . . ויער אלהים את רוח מלך ישמעאלים . . . ויצר על ירושלים (*Taḥkemoni*, ed. P. de Lagarde [Göttingen, 1883], 121). None of these examples, nor the biblical usages (*supra*, n. 143), provide either parallel or precedent for Abravanel's rather glib application of the Cyrus phrase to Ferdinand and Isabella.

I am aware, of course, that the phrase can have a variety of resonances, not all of them necessarily messianic, depending upon the context. At times its use seems merely a reflection of the general medieval penchant for ascribing historical events to the agency of God. For example, in writing of the outbreak of the civil war in Castile between Henry of Trastámara and Pedro the Cruel, the fourteenth-century Jewish author Menahem ben Zerah observes: ויהי בשנה ההיא העיר ה' את רוח מלך דון אנדריק בן המלך דון אלפונשו וילחם עם אחיו דון פידרו (*Zedah la-derekh*, Sabbioneta, 1567, fol. 16; Neubauer, *Medieval Jewish Chronicles*, II, 244). Even Abravanel's own linking of "the Lord stirred up the spirit" to "Asmodai, chief of the demons" (i.e. Ferdinand of Aragon, in the censored passage of his *Comm. on Deut.* cited *supra*, n. 135) might be glossed over as mere hyperbole. Such is not the case, however, with his commentary on Isa. 43. The explicitly messianic character of the entire passage, and the fact that the Cyrus phrase is twice repeated, indicate that the use of the phrase is not at all casual, and deserves our careful attention.

(145) Abravanel, Int. to *Comm. on the Bk. of Kings*. That, by and large, the Spanish exiles continued to accept the leadership of the courtier class is rightly stressed by Ben-Sasson (*Zion*, XXVI, 28–34).

Expulsions, however, were one thing, forced conversions an entirely different matter.

Of all that has been said thus far concerning expulsions, nothing is applicable to baptism by force. We have seen that, with the solitary exception of Ibn Verga, the mild treatment of Ferdinand of Aragon in Jewish sources does not extend to Manuel of Portugal. For although by common consensus kings had the right to expel their Jews, not even the most fervent proponents of royal prerogative, nor canon law itself, acknowledged any royal right to impose Christianity upon the Jews against their will. The forced mass conversion of 1497 was simply illegal by all standards, and Samuel Usque presents not merely a Jewish view when he characterizes it as "this violence, contrary to divine and human laws."[146] The Portuguese themselves had mixed feelings about it from the beginning, and some, like the bishops of Algarve and Funchal, D. Fernando Coutinho and D. Diogo Pinheiro, did not hesitate to brand it a tragic error.[147] Though there is no protest recorded from the papacy at the time, some three decades later Clement VII went so far as to concede, at least regarding the original converts of 1497, that "those should not be considered members of the Church who were forcibly baptized, and they would have every right to complain of being corrected and punished as Christians in violation of the principles of justice and equity."[148] Despite their inevitable post-factum rationalization of the great conversion, such major chroniclers of the reign of Dom Manuel as Osorio and Damião de Góis did not shrink from giving faithful and heart-rending descriptions of the event, in which their sympathies are clearly with the victims.

For Ibn Verga, as for countless others, the Portuguese conversion must have been even more traumatic than the expulsion from Spain. Moreover, for one so prone to ponder the fate of Jewry among the nations it surely posed, beyond its immediate personal implications, a radical challenge to all prior conceptual frameworks. While his faith in the royal alliance had remained

(146) Usque, *Consolaçam*, III, 30v (ed. Cohen, 204); Osorio, *De reb. Emm.* (*supra*, n. 87); Imanuel Aboab, *Nomologia* (Amsterdam, 1629), 298: "O qual Ley Divina, o Humana, Gentilica, o Moderna, permite que se fuercen los animos (que el summo Señor crió libres) á creer lo que no creen, y amar lo que aborrecen." In *Shebet Yehudah*, Ch. 4 (cf. *supra*, n. 129) the Jews say to Ibn Tumart: "Thou art lord of our bodies and king over our money, but He who gave us our souls and will finally restore them to Himself is the King who will judge them . . ."

(147) See the texts of Coutinho's letters published by G. Heine in *Allgemeine Zeitschrift für Geschichte*, IX (1848), 178–80. For Pinheiro see Herculano, *Inquisição em Portugal*, I, 224 f. (299 f. in the English tr.).

(148) Clement's bull "Sempiterno regi," in *Corpo Diplomático Portuguez*, II, 431.

firm even in the face of the Expulsion, how could it be salvaged after the debacle of 1497?

Though we can have no direct access to Ibn Verga's thoughts in the ensuing years, I venture to suggest that it is precisely in terms of this question that the events of 1506 and 1507 may have been of decisive significance to him. In other words, the massacre and the subsequent actions of the king may well have vindicated, as he saw them, not only his conception of the forces which determine Jewish destinies, but the validity of the royal alliance itself.

In Ibn Verga's mind the New Christians were, quite simply, Jews, and that, of course, is how they were still regarded by most of the Portuguese. (We may also recall the German traveller's natural equation of *newen christen oder Juden*.) The massacre of 1506 was thus a massacre of Jews, and the details were less important than the overall configuration. From what he knew, Ibn Verga easily abstracted those elements which struck him as significant and, merely by a few omissions and subtle modifications, he could offer a remarkably vivid proof of his main theses. Some of the distortions we have noted were deliberate. Given his propensity to view events in a certain way, others may well have been unconscious. Above all, the juxtaposition of the various elements results in a narrative which ties together many of the major strands in the *Shebet Yehudah* as a whole. Whatever doubts or confusion the forced baptism of 1497 may have aroused in him, the Lisbon massacre and its aftermath suited Ibn Verga's archetypes to perfection.

This becomes fully evident as soon as we break the narrative in Chapter 60 into its component parts and provide some obvious exegetical comments. Thus:

a) *A pogrom erupted while the king and his court were away from the city.* (Woe to the Jews when the king is not present!)

b) *Its immediate cause was religious hatred and fanaticism* (the uproar over the discovery of the Passover celebration; the "miracle" in the convent and the inflammatory sermons of the friars).

c) *It was the work of the mob and the rabble* (the lower classes, in the absence of royal restraints, are ever ready to attack the Jews).

Thus far Ibn Verga has essentially allowed the facts to speak for themselves. However—

d) *The Jews were themselves partly to blame.* There was also a social and economic grievance, as demonstrated by the Mascarenhas episode. Indeed, "some said that *all* [!] the Christian hatred was due to their hatred of a Jewish tax-collector named Mascarenhas, because he was arrogant toward them and proliferated laws against them." Here we have Ibn Verga at his most characteristic. The Portuguese chroniclers, we recall, did not mention Mascarenhas at all. The German discussed him in detail and emphasized his unpopularity, but at no time did he even hint that he was the *cause* of the massacre. Ibn Verga alone goes out of his way to suggest, gratuitously, that the outbreak may have been due entirely to the hostility which Mascarenhas had provoked by his behavior, and to "prove" this with the assertion that the slaughter ceased when he was killed. We have seen that this was not what actually occurred. Mascarenhas serves Ibn Verga as a foil to demonstrate his repeated assertion that the Jews (here "a Jew") are often the agents of their own destruction. The fact that he presents his theory concerning Mascarenhas as hearsay is merely a blind, as it is in similar instances in the book when he hesitates to speak in his own name.[149] But the lesson of the Mascarenhas story is clear. As the Jews of Spain should have avoided exacerbating the feelings of the populace, so the Portuguese New Christians, for their own security, should now do the same.

e) True to form, *the royal officials did everything they could in order to cope with an impossible situation.* While on this score the Portuguese writers are willing to give them the benefit of the doubt, the Jewish chronicler absolutely insists on it. As always, the gentile elite are wholly committed to the protection of the Jews until they are themselves overwhelmed by the power of the mob.

f) Finally, *though the king, being absent, could not prevent the slaughter, he exacted a prompt and fierce retribution once it occurred.* "He came immediately to the city." That, of course, was not true. But since Manuel did send his officials to the city and they were, in effect, his surrogates, was it really stretching the point too far to say that he had come?[150] At any rate, what obviously most impressed Ibn Verga was the punishment itself. Two friars actually burned at the stake, the entire capital deprived of its title—surely such penalties for attacking the Jews (and for Ibn Verga that was, naturally, the only issue) were almost unheard of! In his enthusiasm for the king's reaction Ibn Verga even offered some further embellishments. He probably knew that Manuel had ordered the expulsion of the friars from the Dominican convent. In his narrative the king proposes to demolish it altogether, but is dissuaded by his advisors. He also had to explain why more of the murderers were not executed,[151] and so invented an "imperial law" which allegedly

(149) The closest and perhaps most blatant example occurs in the immediately preceding chapter (no. 59, p. 125). After describing how João II cruelly wrested Jewish children from their parents and deported them to the island of S. Thomé, Ibn Verga observes: "*And some said* that this decree came because the Spanish exiles had promised the king a certain sum of money in order to be received into the kingdom, but in the end many did not pay it, and so this evil and bitter fruit resulted."

(150) Isaac Ibn Faraj also claims that Manuel came to Lisbon (Marx, *JQR* [o.s.], XX, 267).

(151) Ibn Faraj (*loc. cit.*) writes explicitly that forty persons were hanged. This figure

stipulated that only the leaders of a riot could be punished if more than fifty persons were involved.[152] But for this, Manuel would have put to death all who had participated.

Of course a king who so dramatically avenges the murder of Jews is a "gracious king"! And the forced conversion? One can only speculate as to how Ibn Verga dealt with it in his own mind. Perhaps he was able to understand, if not to condone, the political and economic reasons behind the conversion, if not at the time, then in retrospect. Besides, we have already had occasion to emphasize that in Ibn Verga's eyes royal actions are separable and may be judged independently of one another. In the *Shebet Yehudah* he avoided the problem altogether simply by omitting any direct reference to the events of 1497, and this in itself may indicate the degree to which he felt the king had redeemed himself a decade later. To a man of Ibn Verga's temperament and outlook the forced conversion could now well appear as an aberration, terrible to be sure, but still untypical of the king's behavior both before and after. As a matter of record, Manuel's treatment of the Jews prior to 1497 was quite favorable. Once the conversion was effected, his policy toward the New Christians must have seemed equally if not more benign.[153] The royal alliance was thus not ruptured by the conversion; it had shifted under the new conditions to another plane, but preserved its essential features. Given the equation Jew–New Christian, the Lisbon massacre demonstrated to Ibn Verga the continuum in both mob hatred of the Jews and the royal desire to protect them.

Finally, there was the culminating favor displayed by the king—the edict of 1507 which allowed the New Christians to emigrate from Portugal. After this abrupt reversal of the policy of the previous decade, what further evidence of Manuel's good will could Ibn Verga require? Short of an actual permit to return to Judaism, which could not be realistically expected under any circumstances, the edict of 1507 represented the farthest step the king could take in making redress for the forced conversion. Ibn Verga himself took advantage of this last act of grace to depart from Portugal. In the *Shebet Yuhudah*, the Manuel of 1497 faded before the image of the Manuel of the subsequent decade, *melekh ḥasid*, a gracious king. . . .[154]

roughly corresponds to the estimates given by others. E.g., Acenheiro (*Chrónica*, 323) has "forty or fifty," while an Ajuda Ms. cited by Herculano (*op. cit.*, I, 150) states that altogether forty-six or forty-seven were executed, thirty-two of them in Lisbon.

(152) For another, even more obviously fictitious "law," cf. *Shebet Yehudah*, p. 65, lines 30–34.

(153) In *Shebet Yehudah*, Ch. 4, there seems to be an oblique reference to Manuel's promise of no inquiry into the beliefs of the converts. See Shohat's note, p. 169, *ad loc.*

(154) In his *Israel en de Volken*, the nineteenth-century Sephardic Dutch poet and con-

If the foregoing analysis of Ibn Verga's attitude toward Manuel has any merit, then its implications transcend the problem of the *Shebet Yehudah* itself. For one thing, it may provide a key to a better understanding of those New Christians who remained in Portugal after 1507.

That even then many of the active judaizers among them did not depart is to be explained, in the first instance, by personal factors. Insufficient funds, difficulty in liquidating assets, possible family ruptures, anxiety over braving the unknown, these and a host of other individual considerations must have inhibited New Christians, as they did Jews in other times and places, from making their exodus while it was yet possible. Still, even while recognizing the human element, we cannot resist wondering why more did not leave. After the massacre of 1506, why did they not see the handwriting on the wall? The tragic consequences for those who remained glare through the hindsight afforded by subsequent events. Under Manuel's successor, D. João III, laws of 1521, 1532 and 1535 revived the prohibition against New Christian emigration. In 1536 the Portuguese Inquisition was established, and in 1540 the first victims appeared at an auto-da-fé in Lisbon.

In the *Shebet Yehudah* we find no specific information concerning the fate of the Portuguese New Christians after the massacre of 1506, nor is the permit of 1507 mentioned explicitly.[155] However, Chapter 62 contains certain overtones which cannot be ignored. We read:

vert to Christianity, Isaac da Costa, stated that in some Jewish family traditions Manuel came to be known as the "Jewish king" (cited from the German tr. by Kayserling, *Gesch. d. Juden in Port.*, 154, n. 2). While this is not impossible, Da Costa's failure to indicate a source for his assertion, as well as his own historical biases, render it suspect. However, in attempting to assess the varying aspects of Manuel's image in Jewish eyes, one should also take into account the difference between his conversionist policy within Portugal and the relative lenience which had prevailed from the outset in his overseas possessions, especially in North Africa. There the Jews were neither expelled nor forced to convert, the appointments of chief rabbis continued to be directly confirmed by him, and individual Jews served as his translators and diplomatic agents, some even travelling occasionally to Portugal with a royal license. See the data assembled in my study of "Professing Jews in Post-Expulsion Spain and Portugal," *Salo Wittmayer Baron Jubilee Volume* (Jerusalem, 1974), English Section, vol. II, 1023–58.

(155) However, see Ch. 11 which, though set elsewhere and somewhat garbled, seems to preserve a strong echo of the subsequent situation in Portugal. We read here of widespread persecutions in which multitudes of Jews were baptized. Many tried to leave, "but when it was understood that they intend to go in order to judaize . . . they confiscated their property and money for the king" (p. 56, lines 7–8). Later on, allegedly because of an outbreak of plague (a recollection of the Lisbon plague?) to which they proved immune (!) they were allowed to depart. "Then a great many of the Marranos (אנוסים) went forth to save their souls. But many remained in those lands, afraid lest this [i.e. the permit to

63

In the great city of Seville there lived Rabbi Judah Ibn Verga of blessed memory. When the Inquisition came there the local inhabitants said that if the inquisitors wished to know who are the Marranos who practice Judaism, they should arrest Rabbi Judah Ibn Verga, for it is with his aid that they perform all the deeds and commandments of the Jews. And he, of blessed memory, even before the Inquisition arrived, knew what he would do. He placed in a window three pairs of doves. The first were plucked and slaughtered, and he wrote on their necks—"These shall be the Marranos who are last to leave." The second were plucked but not slaughtered, and he said: "These shall be the middle ones." The others he left with their feathers and alive, and he wrote: "These shall be the first [to depart]." But they did not heed, and so they fell into what befell them. And he passed many Marranos through a fire so that in this way the heavenly decree might be satisfied.[156] He himself then fled and went to Lisbon. There they tortured him severely to make him reveal those who practice Judaism. But he, of blessed memory, stood fast, and died in prison because of the torture. May the merit of all the martyrs stand us in good stead![157]

Since the Inquisition began to function in Seville in 1481, this episode refers to that time, or shortly before. Its legendary and folkloristic element is manifest. But, at its core, it is a tale of how a distinguished member of the Ibn Verga family unsuccessfully warned the Marranos of Seville of their impending doom unless they flee in time. What catches our attention is the specific

emigrate] be a ruse of the peoples to discover what is in their hearts, and these remained in those lands by the thousands."

In the remaining lines Portuguese events are again reflected, but chronologically confused. We are told that those who stayed continued to practice Judaism to the best of their ability, but that subsequently "inquisitors (חוקרים) arose over them to destroy, and began to burn them and confiscate their goods, until a king arose and commanded that no inquisitor shall henceforth be found in his kingdom, nor shall anyone denounce them, for they act in good faith."

If these events are indeed meant to be evocative of Portugal, then the king in question must be Manuel, but the sequence described, in which his promise of immunity *follows* the establishment of the Inquisition is an obvious anachronism. My own feeling is that Solomon Ibn Verga's text has been tampered with by his son Joseph, whose explicit interpolation occurs in the very middle of this chapter (lines 12–18, beginning: "Joseph ben Verga declared . . .").

(156) We seem to have here a strange, quasi-magic ritual, unattested in any other source known to me. The essential idea seems to be that through this symbolic purgation those Marranos will be spared from the fires of the Inquisition itself.

(157) *Shebet Yehudah*, p. 126. Chapter 61, which separates this from the account of the Lisbon massacre, consists of a mere five lines.

location of this chapter in the book. It follows only shortly after the account of the massacre of 1506 (Chapter 60), and immediately before Ibn Verga's final summary of his views on the Jewish question (Chapter 63). Possibly this is mere coincidence. But if, as seems to be the case, the arrangement of the various chapters in the *Shebet Yehudah* is not haphazard, and follows some purposeful order, then we may have here an oblique yet powerful reference to Portugal. Judah Ibn Verga's earlier warning to the Marranos of Seville would serve here as Solomon Ibn Verga's warning to the Portuguese New Christians to flee while they can. The parallel is brought even closer by a further link, the alleged torture of Judah Ibn Verga in *Lisbon*. In other words, we must seriously entertain the possibility that although Solomon Ibn Verga's personal faith in Manuel was fully restored, he was at the same time sufficiently perceptive to conclude that the king's good will might not be sufficient to guarantee safety in the future. In this context we would do well to recall again, but in a more compelling way, the words which Ibn Verga placed in the mouths of the French Jews in 1315—*What gain is there in the benevolence of the king . . . if the will of the peoples is not with us, and they continually seek our ruin?*

The events of 1506 had sustained Ibn Verga's confidence in the Crown. But they had also confirmed, not only his distrust of the mob, but his oft-repeated awareness that where "the will of the peoples" is completely inimical to the Jews, their position may become untenable despite the Crown. One cannot help wondering, however, if many of the New Christians who chose to remain in Portugal after 1507 had not deduced only a partial lesson from what had happened. Like Ibn Verga, they too may have renewed their faith in the royal alliance. They too may have come to regard Manuel as a *melekh ḥasid*. But, in contrast to Ibn Verga, they may have been lulled thereby into a sufficient sense of security so that flight from Portugal no longer seemed imperative.

While such an interpretation of the mentality of the remaining New Christians is admittedly speculative, it acquires more plausibility when we observe their behavior during the subsequent reign of João III. It is remarkable how, throughout their protracted struggle to prevent the introduction of the Inquisition into Portugal, the New Christians display classic Jewish modes of dealing with crisis. At every turn, the venerable methods forged by Iberian Jewish leaders in the heyday of the royal alliance are once more operative— lobbying with the king, emissaries to Rome, pleas and bribery. It is the old "*shtadlanut*" all over again; nothing has changed except the arguments. The entire arduous effort, sustained for no less than sixteen years, would have made no sense without an implicit faith in the Crown. To the bitter end, the campaign presumed that ultimately the king would prove to be tractable. As earlier in Spain, so now, few if any seem to have been able to realize that, misguided or not, the interest of the Crown was in irrevocable conflict with their own. Dom João was determined to have his Inquisition, and in the end, of course, he prevailed. Those who had not escaped between 1507 and 1521 were now, in effect, captives of the Crown and, after 1536, of the Inquisition. In a real sense they had been, from the very outset, prisoners of their own archetypes.

Von dem christenlichen Streyt: Edition A
(Bayerische Staatsbibliothek, Munich)

Von dē christenlichen streyt geschehen
im. M̄D. CCCC. vj. Jar zu Lißbona
ein haußstat in portigal zwischen den christen vñ newen christen
oder juden/ von wegen des gecreutzigisten got.

Von dem christenlichen Streyt: Edition C
by permission of the Houghton Library, Harvard University

Appendix A
The German Account

The text of the printed German pamphlet describing the Lisbon massacre was first brought to the attention of modern scholarship when it was published in 1848 by G. Heine ("Beiträge zur Geschichte im Zeitalter der Reformation, aus Spanischen und Portugiesischen Archiven mitgetheilt: II. Die Einführung der Inquisition in Portugal," in W. A. Schmidt's *Allgemeine Zeitschrift für Geschichte*, IX, 171–78.) He did not indicate where he had found the pamphlet, and merely printed the text as an "Anhang" to his study without utilizing its information. His own description of the events of 1506 was based entirely upon the chronicle of Damião de Góis (see his remarks, *ibid.*, 156).

First to make some actual use of the pamphlet for a reconstruction of the events in Lisbon was Meyer Kayserling, from a copy in the Royal Library in Munich (see his *Geschichte der Juden in Portugal* [Leipzig, 1867], 146 ff.). Since then, on the rare occasions when the German account has been mentioned, scholars have relied upon either Heine or Kayserling without bothering to consult the original.

On the basis of the copy he had seen, Kayserling expressed rather severe strictures against Heine's manner of editing the text (Kayserling, *op. cit.*, 146, n. 3: "Dieses sehr seltene in der Königl. Bibliothek zu München befindliche Schriftchen ist mangelhaft und ungenau abgedruckt am Ende des Aufsatzes von G. Heine."). In particular, he discovered two entire passages in the Munich copy which Heine seemed to have omitted. One of these appeared at the very beginning and told of the discovery of the Marrano Passover; in the other, the German expressed his temporary doubts concerning the miracle of the crucifix. With regard to the latter, Kayserling suggested that the omission was deliberate ("Heine hat diesen ganzen Passus, vielleicht nicht ohne Absicht, ausgelassen"), thus implying that Heine was guilty of Christian bias.

While such a conclusion may have seemed natural under the circumstances, it can now be dismissed. Kayserling was simply unaware that there exist at least three variant editions of the pamphlet and that in two of them the passage skeptical of the miracle does not appear at all. If Heine was deficient as an editor, he was so mainly in his decision to modernize, not only the orthography of the entire text, but its syntax and phrasing as well.

It was my initial good fortune to come across two different editions of the pamphlet (designated below as B and C) in the Houghton Library at Harvard University. Both were formerly in the distinguished collection of Judaica and antisemitica assembled by the late Lee M. Friedman of Boston and bequeathed to Harvard in 1957. Subsequent tracking revealed yet another edition (designated below as A) in the British Museum. Finally, I have located copies of all three editions in the Bayerische Staatsbibliothek in Munich.

The form is that of those ephemeral and ubiquitous "relations" which proliferated in sixteenth-century Europe in various languages. Often essentially letters by private persons describing some noteworthy current event, they spread immediate information from one country to another. Printed as pamphlets shortly after they were received, they were, in effect, the ancestors of the modern newspaper.

Our analysis of the text of the German report has already shown it to have been written almost immediately after the Lisbon massacre, that is, in the last week of April, 1506. Though none of the three publications of the account bears a date or place of printing, all were probably printed within a short time of one another, early in 1507. (The edition we have designated as A actually begins: *In kurtzvergangē jaren . . .*) The orthography is different in each edition, and Ed. A also contains syntactical variations, perhaps an indication that each pamphlet was printed at a different press.

For bibliographic purposes the three editions may be described as follows:

Edition A: (British Museum, 4515.b.8.
Bayerische Staatsbibliothek, 4° H. Eccl. 761)

Von dem christēlichē/ Streyt, kürtzlich geschehen zu Lissbona, ein Haubtstatt/ in Portigall, zwüschen den Christen vnd Neüwen Chri/sten oder Juden, von wegen des Gecreützigten Gottes./ [*Woodcut*]

4°, 10 pp., Gothic letter.
Signatures: Aii,Aiii,Aiiii

The woodcut on the title-page, enclosed in floriated borders, shows a knight kneeling before the crucified Jesus. The knight's horse in seen at the left.

Edition B: (Houghton Library, *GC5/A100/506v
Bayerische Staatsbibliothek, 4° Port. 23d)

Von dem christēlichen streyt geschehē/ jm. M.CCCCC.vj. Jar zu Lissbona/ ein haubt stat in Portigal zwischen den christen vnd newen chri/sten oder juden, von wegen des gecreutzigisten [*sic*] got./ [*Woodcut*]

4°, 9 pp. Gothic letter.
Signatures: Aiii,Aiiii.

The woodcut on the title-page was obviously executed expressly for the pamphlet. It depicts a scene from the Lisbon massacre which contains some of the key elements. *Upper right*: The miraculous crucifix in the Convento de S. Domingos, one man standing, another kneeling in adoration. *Upper left*: some armed men at the entrance to a house, perhaps waiting for the New Christians to emerge. Flames are seen in the background. *Center*: two women conversing, perhaps a reminder of the role played by the women in the initial stage of the massacre. *Bottom left*: two corpses are burning, perhaps the two New Christian brothers who were the first to be killed.

Edition C: (Houghton Library, *GC5/A100/506vb
Bayerische Staatsbibliothek, 5/ 4° Germ. g. 197g)

Von dē christenlichen streyt geschehen/ jm. M.CCCCC.vj. Jar zu Lissbona/ ein haubtstat in Portigal zwischen den christen vñ newen christen/ oder juden, von wegen des gecreutzigisten [*sic*] got./ [*Woodcut*]

4°, 9 pp., Gothic letter.
Signatures: Aii,Aiii.

In the large woodcut on the title page God is on His throne, His right hand pointing to Jesus on the cross, seen in a cloud of mist or smoke. Foreground: two bands of angels, one kneeling, the other standing, face each other. The iconography may relate to Isaiah 6, christologically interpreted.

I have attempted to establish the sequence of these editions on the basis of several considerations. Ed. C was almost surely printed after A and B since, beside other variations, it contains some later information at the end not present in the others. The material contained in Eds. A and B is identical, but I have sought a clue to the order of their printing in the illustrations on their title-pages. Only in Ed. B do we have a woodcut whose details relate specifically to the Lisbon massacre, and I would assume that it took at least some time to commission and execute it. The woodcut in Ed. A, however, which shows a knight kneeling before a crucifix, has no vital connection to the events (except for the crucifix itself). It may therefore have been hastily borrowed from an existing block used earlier in another publication. Such a determination is, of course, admittedly tenuous, since the same remarks can be applied to the woodcut in Ed. C which was, as we have noted, clearly issued after the others.

The three editions of the German account that we have uncovered may not be the only ones that appeared. This can be inferred from internal evidence. Eds. A and B end with the speculation that 1,930 New Christians had perished in the massacre. To this, Ed. C adds two further passages: The first changes the estimate to 1200 and emphasizes that it is difficult to obtain exact figures. The second relates that the king has sent three powerful persons to Lisbon to punish the culprits, especially the friar who ran about with the crucifix, but that the latter has not yet been apprehended. Stylistically, the endings of these two passages indicate that they are independent and were probably written by the German in separate and successive letters as addenda to his original report. Thus the first passage ends: *Also habt ir was sich in Lissbona verloffen hat vom xvii tag des Aprillen biss xxix dicto das mir wissen ist, do mit helff vns got allen.* If, as seems plausible, each letter from the German was printed upon receipt, there may well be an as yet unknown edition which ended at this point, and which appeared between the editions we have designated as B and C. Indeed, it is quite conceivable that there was an edition preceding both A and B, which concluded with the words: *dann was weyter aussgericht wirt, werdt ir zu seiner zeyt wol vernemmen,* which occur in Eds. A and B before the last line and which may therefore have closed the very first letter that the German had sent. By the same token, we cannot exclude the possibility that the promise at the end of Ed. C (*Wass sich weyter begibt, werdt ir zu seinem zeyten vernemen*) was fulfilled, and that there was even a subsequent edition after this.

Some questions remain as to which editions Heine and Kayserling actually consulted. The title given by Heine corresponds to that of Ed. A, though the text does not. The opening paragraph is missing, and the rest of the text has been modernized. Discounting the latter aspect, it is highly probable that this was indeed the edition which Heine utilized.

Kayserling's quotations pose a more interesting problem. His title is that of Ed. A (with the sole difference of *zwischen* instead of *zwüschen,* which may simply be a lapsus), whereas his text is that of Ed. C, quoting the passages that are absent in both A and B. One would conclude from this that either Kayserling misquoted the title or that we may have here an indirect confirmation that yet another edition exists, which combines these features but which has not yet come to our attention. Regrettably, neither Heine nor Kayserling saw fit to mention or describe the woodcuts in the copies they had at their disposal.

Of the anonymous author himself it is doubtful that anything definite can be known. He may have been a traveler, a merchant, even a ship's captain. His literacy would tend to diminish, though not entirely exclude, the possibility that he had been an ordinary sailor. Whoever he was, he was a keen observer and vivid reporter. Even his anti-Jewish animus was kept within bounds sufficient to enable him to retain a measure of objectivity concerning the events themselves. The place of printing of the pamphlets is almost as hard to ascertain as the identity of the writer. For its own copy of Ed. A the British Museum Catalogue suggests M. Hupfuff, Strassbourg, presumably on some typographical evidence. In any case, the pamphlet seems to be of the utmost rarity no matter what the edition, and I have found no mention of it in any bibliography of German *Flugschriften* I have consulted.

The text I now publish is that of Edition C. Passages not found in Editions A and B are enclosed in brackets. Any other significant variants, except those of spelling or phrasing, are noted below. Slashes are reproduced as commas. The orthography reproduces that of the original.

Von dem christenlichen Streyt: Edition C, *Text*

[*Fol. 1r*] Als man zalt nach Christi geburt. 1506. Jar,[1] In Lissbona am. xvii. tag im Aprill was. viii. tag nach dem heyligen karfreytag do wurden dauor begriffen vill newer christen in eynem hawss, die heten zu der österlichen zeyt gemacht brot, auch etlich lemmer, auch hennen getödt vñ zugericht auff jr judisch art, vñ assen vmb zwo vhr in die nacht jr osterlamp vñ hielten also jr Ceremonias auff judisch, vñ einer vnder in der gieng hin heimlich vñ verrieth sie, vñ bracht mit im ein richter võ der stat mit etlichen vil schergen, vñ kamen in das hauss vñ begriffen die essende ob warer that, vñ fiengen jr. xvij. weyb vñ man der die andern fluhen oben zu den decheren hin auf, auch wo sie sunst darvon mochten komen, die andern. xvij. furt man in die gefencknuss. Do wardt als baldt dem kunig geschriben, der was nicht zu Lissbona, sunder in einem stetlein. xxiiii[2] meyl võ Lissbona, genant Brantes, wie man es mit den gefangen halten solt, nit weyss ich was der kunig zu antwurt gab, dañ in.ij tagen nach dem sie gefangen waren liess man jr etlich auss, war gesagt sie weren vnschuldig auss vrsachen, sie villeycht gelt oder sunst gut freundt hetten die in auss hulffen, Do wardt under der gemein heimlich ein gross mürbeln, vnd gesagt sie weren werdt das man die gefangen vñ ander die solchs theten oder verhengten alle verbrent wurden.

Item[3] in Lissbona in einer kirchen genant sant Dominicus besetzt munchen desselben ordens, auff der rechten hãdt in derselben kirchen ist ein grosser altar, vñ in der tafel auff dem altar ein crucifix und ein gitter vor dem crucifix, vnd voren bey dem hertzen in das crucifix gemacht ein spigel, do wurdt ein gemeiner rüff in der kirchen vnd in der gantzen stat gesagt wie das man in

---

(1) Ed. A (begins instead): In kurtzuergangē jaren in Lissbona . . .
(2) A and B: xiiii.
(3) G. Heine's edition of the text begins here.

demselben spigel het gesehen vnser frawen knyent vor unserm herren vnd gewaynt, mer hat es oben in demselben altar vil gulder stern, derselben etlich geleucht haben, auch grösser und kleyner worden, auch liecht oder ander scheyn zuzeyten geschinen soll haben, vnd gechlingen wider erloschen. Mer soll in demselben spigel zu mermal geschehen sein worden ye zwey liechtlein recht brinnen, vñ ye ein gross dicks liecht, solichs hat gewerdt vom karfreytag an biss am Mitwoch nach dem Suntag Quasimodogeniti, was der Mit- [*fol. iv*] woch vor sant Jörgen tag, vñ altag gieng gross mechtig volck do hin walfarten mit besundern procession das wunderzeyhen zu sehen.[4] [Ich bin auch do gewest, hab aber kein scheyn gesehen, auch keyn liechtlein, aber ich hab es wol von cc. personen gehört, vnd von vil meiner guten freundt den wol zu glauben ist, die solchs zu mer mal gesehen haben, die liecht vnd stern scheynen vñ leuchten hab sie auch gefragt ob sie nicht meinten das es gemacht ding von den munchen oder andern were, als man dañ solich buberey wol machen kan, sagten sie vnd meynten gentzlich das das rechtuertig und ein zeychen von got were.]

Item an dem Suntag Quasimodogeniti, drey vhr vngeuerlich nach mittag vor vesper zeyt, am. xix. tag im Aprillen do was aber vil volcks von man vnd weyben in der vorgemelten kirchen die wunder zeychen zu sehen, do waren etlich new christen auch in der kirchen vñ sahen zu vñ horten das die man vñ weyben von disen wunder zeychen sagtē, do was einer võ den newen christen der sagt zu den mannen vñ weyben offentlich, was möcht ein dür holtz wunder zeychen thun, nempt wasser vñ netzt es so sol es als erleschen, do waren die weyben zornig auff in, griffen in an do mit sie denselben fur die kirchen thur brachten, vñ vor der thur haben die weyber an disen zu schlahen vñ rauffen angehoben, sprechende Solstu wider ein solchs gross wunder zeychen vnd crucifix reden, vnd schlugen die weyber den man schier zu todt, do kamen etlich man vnd buben die den weybern hulffen, do mit sie disen gantz todten vnd brachten in auff ein grossen platz vor der kirchen, do kam ein ander newer Christ oder Jud darzu, der dan gesehen das man den andern vnbracht het, vnd sprach. Warumb tödtent ir disen man, sagt das volck, Du bist freylich auch der schelck einer, vnd huben in die buben vnd man an zu rauffen vñ schahen biss sie in auch zu todt schlugen, vñ wolten sie darnach alle bed auff dem platz verbrennen. In dem do kam der Richter einer von der stat mit vil schergen, vermeynt die zu fahen die solch that gethan hetten, do wider was die gantz gemeyn, sagten sie heten recht gethan Nach dem der kunig die Juden oder newen christen nit straffen wolt, so must sie got straffen, vñ sagten im was die Juden gesagt heten, wolt sich der

---

(4) A and B omit the following bracketed passage.

richter daran keren sunder die ander zu fahen do sagt die gemeyn das er
gedecht vñ liess sie ir ding schaffen oder [*fol. 2r*] sie wolten auch uber in, wan
sie marckten das er den Juden auch bey wolt steen, wolt sich der richter
nit daran keren, sunder die fahen do schrey die gãtz gemein schlacht todt
wan dise wöllen den Juden beystant thun, vnd luffen alle uber den richter vnd
schergen, das der richter mit gewalt die flucht in sein hauss must geben vñ
die gemeyn wolt in todt haben, also flohe er zu dem dach oben auss, do mit
er hin wegk kam, do was die gemeyn im willen, wolt im das hauss abbrent
haben In solchem kam das geschrey in die gantzen stat vñ yederman legt
sein harnasch an vñ sein were zu im schreyendt in einer gemein. Wir wöllen
hewt got zu hilff nemen vnd dem christen glauben beystan vnd beschirmen,
vnd die hundt oder Juden alle zu todt schlahen vñ verbrennen, vnd teylten
sich do auss, do lx. auff ein ander ort. c. auff ander örter mer oder minder,
damit ob. x. tawsent man, weyb, vnd kindt die alle in der stat vmb luffen
den gantzen Suntag vnd die gantzen nacht, alle die newen christen oder Juden,
weyb vñ man, jung vñ alt, was sie an kammen auf der strosse, in hewsern
oder wo sie es zu wegen mochten bringen, das todten sie, etlich namen sie
gefangen vnd brachten sie auff sant Dominicus platz, do het man ein fewer
gemacht do wurff mans lebendig ein, vn was todt was in den hewsern vñ
auff der strass name die jungen buben vnd bunden in strick an die helss, arm,
fuess, vnd schlayfften sie auff der erden mit den stricken biss auff sant
Dominicus platz in das fewer. Wollen etlich sagen das vom Suntag an drey
vhr nach mittag biss montag vmb mittag ob sechsshundert person getödt
sindt worden, Vnd auff sant Dñicus platz sindt gewesen zwen gross hauffen
võ den todten ob vierhundert person die do lagen vnd brunnen, so waren sunst
in der stat vill ander fewer do man auch die todten vnd lebendigen cörper
verbrennet.

Item am montag kam ich in Lissbona dingk zu sehen, sag ich furwar das
ich dingk sach das vnglewblich zu sagen oder zu schreyben ist der es selbs
nit gesehen hat von grosser grawsamkeyt wañ ich sach drey munch in der
stat vmb lawffen, zwen von sant Dominicus orden vnd sunst ein, renten
yetzlicher mit einem creutz vnd schreyen, misericordia misericordia, wer dem
christen glauben vñ dem creutz wol beystan der kum zu vnss wañ wir wollen
fech- [*fol. 2v*] ten wider die iuden vnd alle zu todt schlahen, vnd lieff ein
yegklicher an ein besunder ort in der stat mit einer grossen menigk des volcks
das dem creutz nach volget vñ was sie vnder wegen von iuden an kamen man
vnd weyb jung vnd alt reych vnd arm, das must alles sterben vñ luffen in
alle hewser do iuden wonten auch do sie meinden do sie sich verborgen heten,
do brachen sie die thür fenster vnd decher mit gewalt auff, vnd suchten in
allen orten vnd wo sie ein Juden oder Judin, wie vor steet begriffen, die

fiengen sie vnd furtens todt oder lebendig in das fewer auch luffen etlich christen weyber vmb die hulffen die iuden fahen, tödten vnd verbrennen, sie spechten sie auch auss wo sie verborgen lagen, dañ yederman wolt die iuden todt haben.

Item an dem Suntag vor geschriben luff der meyste tayl des volcks in ein grosse gassen, do die kauflewt des meyst tayl innen wonten fur eins iuden hauss mit namen Johañ Roderigo maskarenus, der ist gewesen das haubt võ allen iuden, vol aller buberey betrigerey, falsch, bösslystig, das nicht zu schreyben ist was er sein tage von aller bössheyt vnd buberey ertracht vnd getriben hat, wañ im kein dingk zu vil gewesen ist, das aller menigklich von im gesagt haben vñ noch vil mer dañ man sagen oder schreyben mag vnd do sie dem obgemelten Johañ fur sein hauss kamen do was er der newen zeytung das man die Juden zu todt schulg innen worden, vnd het sein hauss zu geschlossen vnd alle thür verdarlast vnd an allen örten auff das best vermacht der hoffnung als baldt hinen komen solten vnd er stundt oben an dem fenster, vnd sagt zu dem gemeynen volck ir buben ir verreter ir hundt, wen sucht ir, oder was wolt ir, meint ir mich vnd ander newe christen zu fahen vnd zu todten, ich wil noch machen das man ewer zehentawsent muss hencken vnd zeyget den christen die feygen, vnd ir zu spoten vnd zu fluchen, vnd die weyl sich soliche rede verloffen het, do hub die gemeyn an umb sein hauss zu sturmen, do er soliches sach do machet er sich oben zum dach auss darvon ee die gemeyn die pforten auff brechen kundt von dem wüst so vber all vermacht was, die weyl was er hinweg das nieman west wo hin biss auff den affter montag zwo stundt nach mittag, do kam er herfur an einem ort heyst bey der kleynen Juderey auss einem stall meynet [*fol. 3r*] man do er pferdt innen hette hinder einer kirchen heyst sant Juliana nit weyt von dẽ stat thor, vermeynt er so auff das pferdt kem wölt wol darvon komen, vnd vnder wegen kamen vier man zu im, sagten, weyst du nit das dich alle welt sucht zu fahen vnd zu tödten, saget er schweyget lieben freundt vnd helfft mir darvon, ich wil euch geben tawsent duckaten oder was ir haben wölt helft mir nur mit dem leben daruon vnd beleydt mich biss geen sancta Maria de paradiso, ist ein kirch gleych vor der stat, do was des kuniges gubernator, ist der oberst nach dem kunig, der die stat regiret, der het bey im bey vier hundert man, vnd wo der maskarenus do hin komen were, so wer er mit dem leben daruon komen das dañ got nit wolt sollichs geschehen, also wardt der von den vier mannen nit weyt gefurt, vnd bey sant Juliana kirchen do beschrey in ein iunges kleins meydlein, vnd rüfft vberlawt zu dem vierden mall, do geet der maskarenus, nun hete er sich verkleydet das man in nicht wol kennen kundt, do kam ein weyb die riss im sein deck oder duch vom kopff, als hie zu tragen gewonet ist, vnd schrey auch zu mer malen vber lawt das ist der maskarenus, vnd machet ein geschrey das alle welt zu lüff, vñ einer von den vieren der setzt im ein blechens hewblein auff, vnd rucket ims fur das angesicht, do mit man in nit kennen solte, vnd er het sich gantz verkleydt, halff in aber alles nicht, das volck lüff zu vnd wolten in nür todt haben, sagtē die vier ir solt im pein an thun wañ so man als baldt erstech, wurdt ein gross murblen vnder dem volcke, wir wöllen in zu gefangen furen zu dem gubernator, wañ vnder dem gemeynen volck einer wolt in gefangen haben der ander todt, do sprang einer herfur der sprach, Ich glaube in got nicht wañ diser Judt weyter gefurt wirdt, er muss sterben dañ solt er weyter gefurt werden, so wurdt er mit dem leben daruon komen, das wöll got nit, vnd hieb im alssbaldt ein grosse wunden in das angesicht darnach einer nach dem andern die vier hetten in gern beschutzt es war aber keyn beschutz da noch verhanden, sunder yederman lüff zu, man vnd weyb, jung vnd alt in zu sehen, vnd todt zu schlahen, das geschach in einer gassen genant differia, hinder einer kirchen heyst sancta Maria de Concepcion, do man in dan zu todt schlug. Vnd also todt schleyfften sie in herfur auff die rwa noua, [*fol. 3v*] do lüff alle welt zu als ob es das wunderbarlichst ding were das man ye gesehen hette, dañ yederman zu luff in zu sehen vnd tödtten, vnd alle welt stach vñ hieb im nach seynem leyb, wer im nicht ein besundern stich vnd hieb gab der meynt er kundt nit selig werden, vnd rüffet alle welt, hie ist der maskarenus, vnd schleyfften in fur sein hawss, vñ menigklich volget im nach mit grossen freuden einer nam ein stuck von seiner hawss thür, der ander ein stuck von seinem sessel, stüll, banck, oder bette, was er begriffen oder finden mocht in do mit zu verbrennen, vnd schleyfften in biss auff sant Dominicus platz, vnd vnder wegen meret sich das volck, hieben vnd stachen stetz nach seinem leyb, frolockten vnd jubilierten alle die das horten oder sahen.

Item ee man in fieng do waren unser etzlich theutsch vor sant Dominicus kirchen vnd sahen so vil tödter cörper do ligen, die alle obeinander verschmort hetten nicht genüng holtzs, do sagten wir theutschen zu einander, es sol ein yegklicher hundert pfenning geben vmb holtz, die iuden zu verbrennen, das dañ geschach. Vnd gleych do man das holtz bracht auff den platz, in dem do bracht man Johann Roderigo maskarenus, vnd warff in in das holtz oder fewer das wir theutschen gekaufft hetten, do must er mit vnserm holt[z] verbrent werden, des wir dañ all von hertzen fro warn vnd hetten nit gross darfur genomen, dann wir theutschen haben im das fewer vnd todt offt so wol, biss es war ist worden, got sey gelobet.

Item am Erichtag kam der gubernator vnd resator fur die stat als ir vor vernumen habt mit vill volcks vnd liess aussrüffen, alle die dem kunig trew weren vnd bey wolten steen, die solten zu im komen, also das er vngefeer bey vier tawsent man vor der stat zusamen bracht, vnd hüb an su sagen vnd sprach, wir wöllen in die stat, vnd alle die in dem spill mit den Juden sein die wöllen wir fahen vnd straffen nach dem sie verdient haben, vnd gab der gemein trutzig wort, auff meynung als wolt er sie all lassen tödten, gab im die gemeyn die zu im was kommen zu antwort. Herr wir wollen dem kunig trew sein vnd im beysteen mit allem dem das im not thut vnd recht ist, wir wöllen aber wider vnsern herren christū vñ wider das crutz so in der stat vmb geet die vnglaubigen [*fol. 4r*] vnd iuden tödten nit wider in oder sie thun, sunder dē kunig trew sein vñ von des crucifix wegen sterben vnd wider die vnglaubigen streyten, fechten, vnd sie tödten, dañ das ist ein geschick von got der wil die vnglaubigen straffen, darumb herr wir wöllen als das thun das ir vnss von des kunigs wegen heyst, vnd dem kunig bey standt thun, allein wider das crucifix wollen wir nicht fechten in keinen weg, noch niemant fahen, sunder wer dem crucifix widerstandt will thun der muss wider vnss auch thun, vnd wöllen dem crucifix beysteen als lang wir vnser leben haben, aber wen ir wider das crucifix nit wölt sein oder thun so wöllen wir euch beystandt thun in allem das ir vnss heyst oder gebeit, darumb besecht was ir vnss heyst oder thun wölt. Do der gubernator das verman do wardt er zornig, vnd setzt noch mit vil hefftigern worten an sie vnd saget, so hör ich wol das ir dem kunig nit bey wolt steen, sunder nüt morden, rawben vñ stelen wölt, sag ich euch das man soll euch die solchs thun alle hertigklich an leyb vnd gut straffen, saget die gemein wir wöllen nit stelen noch rauben, sunder dem crucifix beystandt thun vnd die iuden helffen vmbbringen, vñ wo ir oder ander wider das crucifix thut, soll wir euch vñ alle die wider das creutz thun vnd die genigen so wider vnss sein fahen vñ tödt schlahen, vnd vnss weren auff das best wir mögen. Do der gubernator hört vñ sache das nit helffen mocht, vñ sich villeycht auch besorgt sie möchten vber in fallen vnd todt schlahen, do sagt er zu der gemein. Ich bit euch ir wölt doch auff hören vnd ewern zorn nach lassen, vnd so ir doch nit auff wölt hören, so geet hin vnd tödt die iuden, stelt vnd rawbt nit, dan das golt vnd gut gehört dem kunig zu, vnd gab der gemeyn gute wort, dañ er sache das nicht anderst helffen wolt. Also die weyl der gubernator mit der gemeyn redet schickt er ein botten nach den andern in die stat zu den munchen, vnd bitten das sie kurtz ab das creutz in die kirchen theten vnd nit mer mit im in der stat vmb lüffen oder das volck damit zusamen samelten vnd ein auffrür in der stat machten wider den kunig vnd die iuden, vnd das gedechten von stund an das sie das theten, vnd der gemein sagten vñ predigten das sie nun auff horten es were genug, vnd das man fridt hielt, vnd wo die munich das nit wölten thun vnd darob sein das solchs geschehe, so het er ein gross volck versamelt, vnd wer in kürtz vom kunig ein suɱ volck zu warten [*fol. 4v*] wölt er hinein in die stat ziehen vñ sie all fahen vñ hencken lassen, vnd do die munich solch vernamen

78

sagten sie es von stund an der gemein, vnd rüfften die gemein an, sprechent. Alle die gut christen sindt die steen hewt vnd alle zeyt dem creutz bey, wir wöllen vnss mit dem gubernator schlahen, wen er vnss was thun wil, vñ machten sich alle zu dem creutz, schrien, vñ fielen auff die knie, alle vber lawt sprechent vnd rüfften, misericordia, wir wöllen hewt dem christen glauben bey steen vñ wider die vnglaubigen streyten vñ fechten, auch wider alle die, die den vnglaubigen bey wöllen steen vnd giengen wider auss die iuden zu suchen vnd zu tödten vñ verbrennen wie vor, vñ wolten vmb den gubernator gar nichts geben sunder beliben vest auff ir meynung, vnd giengen dem tagwerck nach. In dem do dem gubernator die botschafft zu mermalen komen das sich die munich nicht daran keren wolten, do sprach er zu der gemeyn die er bey im het vor der stat, fart hin lieben kinder so ir doch meinem rath nicht volgen wölt, so thut den wenigisten schaden so ir mügt, also gieng die gemeyn von im, do rith er allein heimlich in die stat, in das kloster zu sant Dominicus, vnd bat die munich sie solten nach lassen, nit weyss ich was sie zu antwort gaben dan er macht sich baldt auss dem kloster, kundt nit sehen oder mercken das er vil guts geschafft het, dañ die munich vñ gemeyn irem tagwerck nach giengen wie vor, solchs werdt warhafftig biss man Johañ Roderigo maskarenus verbrennet, do liessens nach, vnd die munich mit irem creutz von sant Dominico in ir kloster, dennocht denselben tag tödet man vnd verbrennet stetz volck, vñ ir etlich schlugen sich zusamen vñ lüffen vor der stat auff den dörffern do dañ vil iuden waren, vñ schlugen ir ein gut teyl denselben abent zu todt, vnd fiengen ir auch vil, die brachten sie denselben abent in die stat, vn bliben etlich von der gemein aldo vor der stat do schlugen sich die pawrn zu in, vnd lüffen mit einander weyter iuden zesuchen vñ zu todtẽ, auch eins teyls rawben. Vñ do der gubernator vernam das sie rawbtẽ, do zug er mit etlichem volck auff die dörffer hin vñ her, vñ wo er begriff lewt die das volck todten oder rawbten, vñ er ein wenigen ein vrsach zu in mocht haben vñ ir möchtig sein, die hieng er an die bawm hin vñ her, vnd liess auss rüffen die er hieng das thet er auss vrsach das er dem pawrn volck ein forcht in wolt iagen vnd in schrecken vnd machen das man in [fol. 5r] forchten solt vnd nicht weyter schaden thun mit rawben, tödten, stelen, vnd hat ir vber acht nit gehenckt auff mer pletzen ein hie her den andern dort, vnd auff andern orten oder pletzen ander zwen oder drey do mit er vmb gantz lissbona ein rüff vñ geschrey in das volck gemacht hat, sprechendt. Der gubernator corifator zyhen im gantzen landt vmb fahen, tödten, vnd hencken alle die die handt gelegt zu stelen, rawben, auch tödten, do mit er wie vor steet der gemein ein forcht in iager auff dem lande, auch in der stat Mer hat er vnd auch ander richter bey funfftzig, etlich wöllen sagen ob hundert man gefangen, die in sollichem schuldig sein, nicht weyss man was der kunig mit in schaffen wirdt, oder wie man sie verurteyln wurdt, dañ es steet noch gantz wildt in Lissbona vnd vmb Lissbona mit der gemeyn vnd dem pawrs volck, dann was weyter aussgericht wirt, werdt ir zu seiner zeyt wol vernemen.

Item man sagt auch das vmb Lissbona nechst vñ in Lissbona von iuden vñ newen christen mangeln sollen. 1930. jung vnd alt, weyb vnd kindt,[5] [aber ich glaub nit das vber tawsent biss in zwelff hundert gestorben sein, ich glawb auch das es noch niemantz anders grundlich wissen kundt, auss vrsach das vil volkcs dẽ sterben geflohen ist, auch sunst etlich daruon geflohen sindt vñ verborgen auss solchen vrsachen gedunckt mich künn man kein grundt nicht wissen eygentlich was man mangelt. Also habt ir was sich in Lissbona verloffen hat vom. xvii. tag des Aprillen biss. xxix. dicto das mir wissent ist, do mit helff vnss got allen.

Weyter ist sieder biss auff dato nichts besunders gehandelt worden, allein der kunig hat drey mechtig von seinem rethen geen Lissbona geschickt sich zu erkundigen wer vrsach des auflauss gewesen sey, auch auss lassen ruffen wer der munich wiss oder beherberigk die mit dem creutz vmb geloffen sindt, der soll sie fahen oder den herren ansagen damit sie gefangen werden, bey grosser peen vnd straff an leyb vnd gut, aber biss her ist den munich noch keyner begriffen worden, man sagt auch sie sollen schon auss dem landt sein. Was sich weyter begibt, werdt ir zu seinen zeyten vernemen.]

(5) A and B end here. The following bracketed passage not in Heine.

Appendix B
The Portuguese Documents

1.

Letter of D. Manuel to Diogo d' Almeida, Prior of Crato;
Ayres da Silva, Regedor da Casa de Suplicaçam;
Álvaro de Castro, Governador da Casa do Civel;
and Diogo Lobo da Silveira, Baron of Alvito
(Évora, April 24, 1506).

Priol, Regedor, Governador, Barão amigos nos El Rey vos enviamos muito
saudor, a nos nos pareceo despois de agora derradeiramente vos termos escrito
por Pedro Correa, que naõ aproveitando ao asento dessa uniaõ as cousas, que
vos mandamos, que nisso fizesseis, alem de logo nos avizardes hum de vos
outros, qualquer que mais despejado for, vaa a Setuval dar rezaõ de todo, o
que he passado, e mais se faz ao Duque com esta nossa Carta, que lhe escrevemos, pola qual lhe encomendamos, que tanto que a elle chegar qualquer de
vos outros, se for, se mude, e venha logo a ribatejo naquelle modo, que lhe
parecer para aproveitar no negocio asi per força, como per geito, e alem disso
mando tambem armar, e fazer prestes todos os navios da dita villa, e de
Cezimbra, que a vos todos parecer que devem ir, de que levara recado aquelle
que for; porem volo notoficamos asi, e vos encomendamos, que naõ se asen-
tando o feito, como dito he, vaa hum de vos outros ao dito Duque meu
Sobrinho a lhe dar de tudo rezaõ para a sua vinda como dizemos, e asi para
o mais dos ditos navios, porque nos parece, que aproveitara muito chegarse
elle para a cidade, em quanto nos provemos no mais que se ouver de fazer;
e indo o Duque, avemos por bem, que a execuçaõ de todas as cousas, que se
ouverem de fazer, fiquem a elle em solido, consultando se com vosco, todos
quatro, e com vosso parecer e conselho, e as dara elle a execuçaõ, porem
esta ida sua avemos por bem, que seja, parecendo vos a vos outros todos
quatro, que he nosso serviço elle aver de ir, e quando asi volo parecer, entaõ
ira hum de vos outros, como dito he, e parecẽdo vos, que sua vinda naõ he
necessaria, e somente avera necessidade dos navios, escrever-lhoeis para enviar
os que vos parecerem, que de la devem vir, e mandarlheeis nossa Carta para
elle por vertude della o fazer, e asi lhe escrevereis a gente que vos parecer,
que nelles deve vir, para tudo logo se fazer prestes, isto se vos parecer, que

os navios saõ necessarios para tolher a entrada, ou fazerem outra couza, que nosso serviço for, e parecendovos, que somente abastara virem de la navios, em taõ lhe escrevereis, e mandareis somente a Carta, em que vay em cima navios, e quando al vos parecer, em taõ ira hum de vos outros com a outra carta, que a tras fica dito, e se navios ouverem de vir de Setuval, manday estas duas nossas Cartas a Simaõ de Miranda, e a Nuno Fernandes pelas quaes lhe encomendamos, que armem cada hum seu navio, e se venhaõ ahi com elles para nos servirem naquellas couzas, que lhe por nosso serviço oredenardes, escrita em Evora, a vinte e quatro de Abril de 1506.

— Jozé Mascarenhas Pacheco Pereyra
Coelho de Mello, *Sentença da Alçada que El-Rei Nosso Senhor mandou conhecer da Rebellião succedida na Cidade de Porto em 1757* (Porto, 1758), 120–23;
Kayserling, *Gesch. d. Juden in Portugal,* 349 f.

2.

Letter of D. Manuel to the Corregedor, Vereadores, Procurador, and Procuradores dos Mesteres (Évora, April 26, 1506).

Corregedor, vereadores, p^{dor} e procuradores dos mesteres, Nos el Rey vos enviamos muyto saudar. Vymos vosa carta de Crença, que nos trouxe lopo dabreu, fidalgo de nossa casa e cidadão dessa cidade, e per vertude della ho ouuymos em todo o que da vossa parte nos fallou, acerqua da ounyam e ffeyto que se fez em esa cidade comtra os xpãos nouos; E neste casso Nos creemos, pello grande desceruiço de ds̃ e nosso que nelle sse cometeo, que o pouo desa cidade Receberya, pello que aella toqua em coussa tam desacostumada, como esta foy a seu grande louuor, E a comta q̃ sempre de sy deram a seu Rey, muy grande desprazer, e nõ permeterya que tall cousa se fezesse em tamto dano de noso seruiço, amtes, quanto nelle fosse, o rremediarya e farya toda sua posybylidade, pero o que atee ora nam fosse dado tam imteyro Remedio como deuya. E pello dito Lopo dabreu nos emvies dizer que vos pareçe q̃ pera de toda sse Remediar, comvyria nos achegarmos p^a la. Nos, pello q̃ ja he feyto, que nam teem Remedio, como tambeem pella indisposisam da saude da cidade, ho leixamos loguo agora de fazer, comfyamdo que essa cidade he abastante p^a Remediar coussa mayor, e que mais importasse a nosso seruiço,

82

posto que esta seja tamanha como he; E p^r tamto vos encomēdamos e mãdamos que vos ajuntes loguo com o prioll do crato, e cõ ho Regedor da casa da sopricaçã, e com o governador e com ho baram, q̃ neste casso la temos mamdado emtemder, e juntamēte com elles prouede neste casso com aquella diligencia e efeyto que ē tall casso se Requere, e como desa cidade ho deuemos confyar, lembramdouos como p^a este e outros muy mayores seruiços o pouo desa cidade teem tamta obrigaçã, como teem pellas merces e fauores q̃ seempre folgamos de lhe fazer, e p^a q̃ seempre aveemos de teer booa vomtade; E quamdo pella vētura o mal deste casso fosse tamto, que pela cidade sse nam podesse de todo apagar e Remediar, o que nam Creemos, Emtam nam soomēte nos chegaremos p^a ella, como nolo rrequeres, mas ētraremos ē pessoa nella, posto q̃ muy mayor pestenença aja, p^a o prouermos segundo a obrigaçã do caso ho Requere: E do q̃ nisso fezerdes, vos teremos muyto ē seruiço loguo nos avisardes pellas paradas, q̃ temos mandado poer.

— E. Freire de Oliveira, *Elementos para a história do municipio de Lisboa* (Lisbon, 1882), I, 395–401; abridged text in *Documentos do Arquivo Histórico da Câmara Municipal de Lisboa*, IV (Lisbon, 1959), no. 105, p. 121.

3.

Letter of D. Manuel to the Prior of Crato, Regedor da Casa de Suplicaçam, Governador da Casa do Civel, and the Baron of Alvito (Evora, April 27, 1506).

Nos El Rey vos enviamos muito saudar. Vimos a Carta que vos Priol e Baraõ nos escrevestes do que tinheis feito no caso da uniaõ dessa cidade, e morte dos christaõs novos della, a que vos enviamos, e do asento e asocego, em que o negocio estava, e o dalguma execuçaõ, que era feita da justiça e prizaõ doutros, que prendera João de Paiva Juiz com outros provimentos, que tinheis feitos em vossa Carta apontados, e com tudo ouvemos muito prazer, e volo agradecemos muito, e confiança temos de vos, que em tudo se fará o que for mais nosso serviço, e pois louvores a nosso Senhor, isto esta asi bem, e asocegado, e se começa a fazer justiça sem mais mover outro alvoroço, nos avemos por bem que na justiça se meta mais as maõs, e que logo mandeis justiça apena de morte ate com pessoas dos que se puderem aver mais culpados no caso, e que sejaõ dinos de semelhante pena lhe ser dada antre os quaes folgaremos, e vos mandamos, que sejaõ vinte ou trinta molheres, porque da uniaõ destar somos enformados que se seguio o mais desta mal que he feito; isto porem parecendo vos que seguramente se pode fazer, e que naõ seguiraõ disso inconvenientes para se mover outro alvoroço, e uniaõ, porque isto deixamos a vossa desposiçaõ, pero parecendo-vos que senaõ deve fazer ainda agora justiça, apontai-nos por escrito as rezoens, porque volo parece, e se todos naõ fordes acordados en hũas rezoens o que tiver parecer contrario para se fazer, ou leixar de fazer, aponte-o por si enviamos tudo para o vermos, e averdes nossa determinaçaõ, porque aqui avemos desperar por vosso recado, e certo que este caso he de qualidade, que nos parece, que se deve fazer nelle esta obra logo agora, e o mais que merece, ficar para seu tempo, e para esta execuçaõ melhor mandardes fazer, parecenos que deveis fallar com os Vereadores, e com os Procuradores dos mesteres e vintequatro delles, e lhe apresentardes a obrigaçaõ que tem para muito deverem folgar deprocurar a justiça deste caso nos culpados pois foraõ e saõ as pessoas que saõ, e que elles se devem trabalhar por os aver a maõ, e os entregar, porque com isso satisfaçaõ a obrigaçaõ, que tem a nossa serviço, e a suas limpezas, com quaesquer outras mais rezoens, que vos bem parecerem; e se para esta obra de justiça, convier entrardes na Cidade; encomendamos vos que naõ tenhais para isso pejo pois tanto releva a nosso serviço, e a reputaçaõ de nosso estado, como vedes, e podeis vos poer na casa de mina, ou em qualquer outro lugar, que vos bem parecer, e nos temos la mandado Gaspar Vas, para recolher a gente da ordenança que tinha, podeis vos nisso aproveitar delle em qualquer outra cousa, em que elle vos possa servir; e nos temos tomado determinaçaõ, que feita esta execuçaõ, que nos avemos muito por nosso serviço se fazer, estando nos ca, nos abalaremos logo para la e mais junto, que pudermos, para privermos no mais que nos parecer nosso serviço, noteficamos volo asi, e vos encomendamos, que logo a todo o contendo nesta carta nos respondais, e com esta vos enviamos huma carta para o Arcebispo, porque lhe mandamos, que se venha logo ahi, enviai lha logo, porque muito aproveitara sua vinda para o socego dos clerigos, e frades polo que nos escrevestes.

Despos desta escrita nos pareceo, que era bem naõ fazerdes nisto da justiça obra alguma, e somente avemos por bem, que logo apressa nos escrevais, e e emvieis acerca disso vosso parecer asi se vos parece, que se deve de fazer, e se fara sem inconveniente algũ, e nos escrevemos a Joaõ de Paiva, que trabalha deprender algum golpe delles, folgaremos de lhe darder para isso toda a ajuda, e favor, que comprir, parecendo-vos, que se pode asi bem fazer, e sem inconveniente algum.

Os frades avemos por bem, e vos mandamos, que logo sejaõ prezos, e os mandeis poer em todo bom recado, ou no Castello, ou em outra parte qualquer, em que possaõ estar seguros, e como forem arrecadados no lo fareis saber, para vos mandarmos a maneira que com elles se ha de ter, e acerca dos Christaõs novos, nos vos tinhamos mandado, quando de ca partistes que os pusesseis em bom recado, e parecemos que naõ os deveis mandar sahir fora da cidade por vosso mandado, porque naõ seria nosso serviço fazer se asi, antes averiamos por inconveniente, e em sua guarda poede qualquer bom recado, que vos parecer, porem querendo se elles sair; sayaõ–se em boa ora, porem para aver de ser per mandado, parecia em alguã maneira fraqueza da justiça, e tambem saindo-se juntos se poderia seguir algum alvoroço, e a reposta desta carta nos enviai a grande pressa, escrita em Evora a vinte sete de Abril de 1506.

— Mello, *Sentença da Alçada*, 123–28; Kayserling, *Gesch. d. Juden in Portugal*, 350–53.

4.

D. Manuel to the Vereadores, Procurador, and Quatro dos Mesteres, ordering them to proceed to Monguelas (*Setubal, May 3, 1506*).

Pero Váz da Veigua e Luis da Costa vereadores e procurador e os quatro dos mesteres da nossa cidade de Lixboa e Nuno Fernandez scripvam da camara da dita cidade . . . Compre a noso serviço vyrdes todos a nos pera comvosco fallarmos algumas cousas. Porem vos mamdamos que loguo tamto que esta vos for dada vos partaes todos juntamente e vos vymde de meenhãa que he quymta feyra a Mongeellas homde avemos por bem que vos venhaes apreseemtar. E como hy fordes fazeynollo saber pera vos mamdarmos omde vos venhaes pera vos fallarmos . . . Scripta em Setuval oje quarta feira ás quatro oras depois meo dia, a iij dias de Março [*sic*!; lege: *Maio*]. Amtonio Carneiro a fez. 1506.

— *Câmara Municipal de Lisboa*, IV, no. 106, p. 122; Oliveira, *Elementos*, I, 401.

5.

Edict of D. Manuel against the City of Lisbon (*Setúbal, May 22, 1506*).

Dõ Emanuel pela graça de Deos Rei de Portugal, & c.

Fazemos saber que oulhãdo nos hos muitos insultos & dãnos que em ha nossa çidade de Lisboa, & seus termos foram comettidos, & feitos de muitas mortes de christãos nouos, & queimamento de suas pessoas, & assi outros muitos males sem temor de nossas justiças, nem reçeo das penas em que comettendo hos taes malefiçíos encorriam, nam esguardando quanto era cõtra seruiço de Deos, & nosso, & contra ho bem, & assossego da dita çidade, visto quomo ha culpa de tam inormes damnos, & malefiçios, nam tam somente carregaua sobre aquelles que ho fezeram, & cometteram, mas carrega isso mesmo muita parte sobre hos outros moradores, & pouuo da dita çidade, & termo della, em q̃ hos ditos malefiçios foram feitos, porque hos que na dita çidade, & lugares estauam se nam ajuntaram com muita diligençia, & cuidado com nossas justiças, pera resistirẽ ahos ditos malfeitores, ho mal, & damno que assi andauam fazendo, & hos prenderem pera hauerem aquelles castigos que por tam grande desobediençia as nossas justiças mereçiam, & que todolos moradores da dita çidade, & lugares do termo em que foram feitos deueram, & eram obrigados fazer, & por ho assi nam fazerem, & hos ditos malfeitores nã acharem quem lho impedisse, creçeo mais ha ousadia, & foi causa de muito mal se fazer, & ainda algũs deixauam andar seus criados, filhos, & seruos nos taes ajuntamẽtos sem disso hos tirarem, & castigarem quomo theudos eram. E porque has taes cousas nam deuẽ passar sem graue puniçam, & castigo, segundo ha diferença, & calidade das culpas que hũs, & outros nisso tem. Determinamos, & mandamos sobre ello com ho pareçer de algũs do nosso conselho, & desembargo, que todas, & quaesquer pessoas, assi dos moradores da dita çidade, quomo de fora della que forem culpados em has ditas mortes, & roubos, assi hos q̃ per sim mattaram, & roubarão, quomo hos q̃ pera has ditas mortes, & roubos deram ajuda, ou cõselho, allẽ das culpas corporaes, q̃ por suas culpas mereçem, percão todos seus bẽs, & fazendas, assi mouẽs quomo de raiz, & lhe sejão todos confiscados pera coroa de nossos Regnos, & todolos outros moradores, & pouos da dita çidade, & termos della, onde hos taes malefiçios foram comettidos que na dita çidade, & nos taes lugares presentes eram, & em hos ditos ajuntamentos, nam andaram, nẽ cometteram, nem ajudaram a cometter nenhum dos ditos malefiçios, nem deram a isso ajuda, nem fauor, & porem foram remissos, & negligentes em nam resistirem ahos ditos malfeitores, nem se ajuntaram com suas armas cõ nossas justiças, & poerem suas forças pera contrariarem hos ditos males, & damnos, quomo se fazer deuera, percão pera nos ha quĩta parte de todos seus bẽs, & fazendas, moués, & de raiz, posto q̃ suas molheres ẽ ellas partes tenhão, ha qual quinta parte sera tambẽ confiscada pera Coroa de nossos Regnos. Outrosi determinamos, & hauemos por bẽ (visto ho que dito he) que da publicaçam desta em diante nam haja mais na dita çidade eleiçam dos vintequatro dos mesteres, nẽ isso mesmo hos quatro procuradores delles, que na camara da dita çidade soiham destar pera entenderem no regimento, & segurança della, cõ hos vereadores da dita çidade, & hos nam haja mais, nem estem na dita camara, sem embargo de quaesquer priuilegios, ou sentenças que tenham pera ho poderem fazer, & bem assi polas cousas sobreditas deuassamos em quanto nossa merçe for ho pouo da dita çidade, pera apousentarem com elles, quomo se faz geralmēte em todolos lugares de nossos regnos, ficando porem ha renda da imposiçam pera se arrecedar, quomo atte agora se faz, per offiçiaes que nós pera isso ordenamos, pera fazermos della ho que houuermos por bē, & nosso seruiço. Porem mandamos aho nosso corregedor da dita çidade, & a todolos outros corregedores, juizes, & justiças a que pertençer, & ahos vereadores da dita çidade, & aho nosso apousentador mór, que assi ho cumpram, & guardem em todo sem duuida, nem embargo que a isso ponhão, porque assi he nossa merçe. Dada em Setuual a xxij dias de Maio de M.D.VI.

— Damião de Góis, *Crónica do felicíssimo rei D. Manuel* (Coimbra, 1939), I, cap. ciii, 256–58.

6.

Edict of D. Manuel Permitting the New Christians to Emigrate from Portugal (*Tomar, March 1, 1507*).

Dom Manoel por graça de Deos, & c. A quantos esta nossa Carta virem: Fazemos saber, que depois do Convertimento dos Judeos de nossos Regnos a a nossa Sancta Fée, por avermos que era mais bem pera sua salvaçam, fizemos Ordenaçaõ, per a qual defendemos sob certas penas, que nenhuns dos Christãos Novos se naõ fossem de nossos Regnos sem nossa licença; e posto que a dita Ordenaçaõ, e defeza fosse feita sem limitaçaõ de tempo, nossa tençaõ porém foi se aver de guardar em quanto nos parecesse, que convinha pera mais seu bem; e por agora nos parecer, que pera a sobredita cousa naõ he necessario a dita defeza mais de haver de guardar, ante avemos por cousa mais proveitosa naõ se husar mais della por tal, que aquelles, que boõs quizerem seer, e estar em nossos Regnos, seraõ por taes conhecidos, e favorecidos, e bem tractados, e recebam de Nós mercês, e favor, como he razam, que lhe seja feita; e aquelles, que boos nam forem, e se quizerem hir, e em nossos Regnos nam estar; pois taes desejos tem, he melhor serem fóra delles que nelles estarem; e por sermos nesta cousa requeridos pelos dictos Christãos Novos, e querendo-lhes fazer graça, e mercê, por esta presente Carta lhe outorgamos, e queremos, e nos praz, que daqui em diante a dita Ordenaçam, e defeza, que lhe tinhamos posta pera dos nossos Regnos, e Senhorios se nam irem sem nossa licença, nam haja mais lugar, e a revogamos, e havemos por nenhuma, e de nenhum vigor, e força; e nos praz, que aquelles,

87

que de nossos Regnos e Senhorios se quizerem hir pera terra de Christãos, o possam livremente fazer, e cada vez que lhe aprouver, assi por mar, como por terra, com suas molheres, e filhos, e todas suas fazendas, sem por ello lhe serem feitos a elles, nem aquelles, que os levarem em suas Naus, e Navios, e assi por terra, costrangimento algum, nem encorrerem em pena algũa.

E aquelles, que se forem, poderaõ tornar a nossos Regnos, e Senhorios livremente quando quizerem, e lhes bem vier, e nelles estar quizerem; e em suas ydas, e vindas nam receberam oppressam, costrangimento, nem sem razam alguma, e seram assi hos que ficarem, como hos que se forem, e despois tornarem, favorecidos, e bem tractados, e em todas suas cousas assi como proprios Christãos Velhos nossos naturaes.

Item revogamos, e havemos por revogada assi mesmo a Ordenaçam defeza, que tinhamos posta, pela qual defendemos, e mandamos, que os ditos Christãos Novos nam podessem vender seus bens de raiz, e queremos, que naõ haja a dita Ordenaçam, e defeza mais lugar, e livremente poderam vender, trocar, escambar todos seus beẽs de raiz, de qualquer calidade de que forem, e fazer delles ho que lhes aprouver, sem por ello encorrerem nas penas de nossa Ordenaçam, e defeza; porque Nós a havemos por nenhũa, e de nenhum vigor, e força, como dito he.

Item nos praz revogar, e havemos assi meesmo por revogada a Ordenaçam, e mandado, porque defendemos, que se naõ fizesse com elles Caimbios nenhũs, e praz-nos, que os possam fazer com quaesquer pessoas, que lhes bem vier, e passar por elles seus dinheiros em quaesquer lugares, que hos ouverem mester pera seus contractos, e para qualquer outra necessidade, pera que lhe sejam necessarios, sem elles, nem has partes, com que hos fizerem, encorrerem por ello nas penas de nossa Ordenaçam, e defeza, que sobrello temos feita.

Item nos praz relevar, e defeito relevamos a todos aquelles Christãos Novos, que destes Regnos se foram contra nossa defeza, e mandado, todalas penas Cives, e Crimes, em que tem encorrido por se hirem contra nossa defeza, e mandado, assi no que tocar a suas pessoas, como fazendas. E estes mesmos, querendo-se tornar para nossos Regnos, e Senhorios, o poderam livremente fazer sem serem costrangidos pelas dictas penas, em que tem encorrido; e querendo nelles assentar, e viver, ho poderam fazer, e seram avidos como se agora á feitura desta Carta em nossos Regnos estevessem pera gouvirem, e husarem de todolo, o que por esta nossa Carta podem gouvir, e husar hos que agora nestes Regnos estam. Porém declaramos, quanto a a pena Civees dos taes, que por quanto poderá seer, que Nós temos feitas mercês dalguns beẽs, e fazendas dos sobredictos a algũas pessoas, que nesta parte se fará comprimento de justiça a as partes, e aquelles, a que has ditas mercês tiverem feitas, usaram por ellas do dereito, que teverem, ou hos sobredictos se concertaraõ com elles, como lhes milhor vier.

Item nos praz desobrigar, e avemos por desobrigados todos aquelles, que temos mandado, que dem fianças pera se nam hirem fóra destes Regnos sem nossa licença; e a aquelles, que has teverem dadas, nos praz, que sejam desobrigados das dictas fianças, e assi todos seus fiadores, e livremente poderam fazer de si o que lhes prouver, e de suas fazendas, e em sua estada, ou partida, ho que lhes milhor vier no modo, que acima lho outorgamos; e de todas, e de cada huma das cousas sobredictas os fazemos livres, e hos desobrigamos, e queremos, e nos praz, que por bem das dictas obrigaçoens, e defezas, que sobre as ditas cousas erão feitas, lhe nom sejam feito costrangimento alguũ.

Item lhe promettemos, e nos praz, que daqui em diante naõ faremos contra elles nenhũa Ordenaçam, nem defezas como gente distincta, e apartada; mas assi nos praz, que em todos sejam avidos, favorecidos, e tractados como proprios Christãos Velhos, sem delles serem distinctos, e apartados em cousa alguma. Porém o notificamos assi a todos nossos Corregedores, Juizes, Justiças, Alcaides, Meirinhos, e todos outros Officiaes, e pessoas, a que esta nossa Carta for mostrada, e ho conhecimento della pertencer, e lhe mandamos, que em todo lhe cumpraõ, e guardem, e façam inteiramente cumprir, guardar, como nella he conteudo, sem lhe irem, nem consentirem hir contra cousa alguma do que por esta lhe outorgamos, ou parte della, porque assi he nossa mercê.

Dada em Tomar a primeiro dia de Março. Antonio Carneiro a fez. Anno de mil e quinhentos e sete.

[*Postscript*]: E esta mercê lhe assi fazemos, para se poderem hir fóra destes nossos Regnos, aquelles que ho quizerem fazer, se entenderá, que elles naõ vaõ, nem se passem em outros Navios, salvo nos dos nossos Regnos, e de nossos naturaes, e não destrangeiros, e com esta limitaçaõ lho outorgamos.

— Joseph, King of Portugal, Decree of May 25, 1773, abolishing all legal distinctions between Old and New Christians (published Lisbon, Regia Officina Typografica, May 27, 1773). [Manuel's edict is printed in an appendix, copied directly from the original document in the Torre do Tombo. With minor differences in orthography the same text appears in a second appendix, comprising the ratification and renewal of Manuel's edict by João III on December 16, 1524.]

7

Letter of the Queen, Dona Maria de Castella, Informing the Lisbon Authorities of Her Efforts to Persuade the King to Revoke the Penalties Imposed Against the City (July 14, 1508).

... [a seus rogos el-rei D. Manuel annuira, e lhe aprazia perdoar e relevar] as cousas comteudas na sentença, que ssobre o casso da uniam dos xpãos nouos sse deu ... averemsse quintar fazemdas aos negrigemtes, E asy nom aver daver hy apossemtadarias, que nom aja hy mais mesteres, nem vimte quatro, nem juizes despritaees como damtes avia; E apraz a sua alteza q̃ as ditas cousas se tornem ao pomto e estado q̃ damtes eram, amte q̃ a sentença fosse dada; E por que saibais como a vontade do dito S^{or} he esta, e como nos polo vosso folgamos de o Requerir e procurar, volo notificamos, pera poderdes mamdar Requerir a sua alteza os despachos e prouissoes que açerqua disso forem necesarios; E aalem do que neste casso fezemos, ssempre folgaremos de Requerir e procurar toda coussa, q̃ seja homrra e crecẽtamemto desa cidade, pola muito boa vomtade q̃ lhe temos, E asy por nos pareçer q̃ ao dito S^{or} fazemos seruiço, Requeremdolhe por esa cidade, em q̃ cabem tamtos merecimentos, e a que sua alteza tamta boa vomtade tem.

— E. Freire de Oliveira, *Elementos para a história do Municipio de Lisboa,* I, 403 f.

8.

Edict of D. Manuel Restoring the Privileges of the City of Lisbon (Sintra, August 2, 1508).

Alvará del Rey D. Manoel em que Concede os Preuelegios, e mais regalias que tinha tirado na oCazião do Leuantamento que nela houve:

Dom Manoel por Graça de Deos Rey de Portugal daquem e daLem Mar em Africa, Senhor de Guine e das Conquistas Nauegação comercio da Etiopia Arabia Percia e da India A quantos esta nossa Carta Uirem, Fazemos Saber que Considerando noz os muitos Grandes aSignados SeruiSSos que aos Reyis paçados e a nos tem feitos a nossa mui Nobre e Sempre Leal Cidade de Lixboa e Pouo della Com muito Amor e Lialdade aSy com muito expargimento do

Seu Sangue Como Com grandes gastos de Suas fazendas e esperamos que daqui em diante fação pelas quais rezois e cada huma delas querendo Noz lhe fazer mercê e agalardoar os ditos Seruiços Como A noz Cabe e em expecial por Noz a Raynha minha Sobre todas muito Amada e prezada Molher pela Cidade muy afectuosamente requerer pela muy Boa Vontade e Amor que lhe Sempre teue, e tem nos Praz e hauemos por Bem que a Sentença que por Noz Com os do nosso Dezembargo, foi dada Contra a dita Cidade e Pouo della por algumas negregencias que por ela paçou, no Cazo da União que se na dita Cidade fez contra os Christãos nouos pela qual lhe houuemos por quebrantadas Suas Liberdades em lhe quitar Suas fazendas e Leuastar que pouzem com elas em Suas Casas, nem OuVerem Vinte e quatro, nem tiuecem Ospritais, nem ConSustorios, nem estiuecem à Menza da Veriação, Como dantes estauão, e porquanto noz por fazer mercê a dita Cidade, pelos respeitos aSima ditos queremos que a dita Sentença Seja em Si nenhuma, e de nenhum Vigor, nem efeito deste Dia para Sempre, e aos ditos Mesteres, e Pouo da dita Cidade lhe sejão Guardadas todas as honrras, e Liberdades e Preuelegios que dos Reyis paçados e de noz Antes da dita Cidade tinhão digo antes da dita Sentença tinhão Sem com eles prezarem, e tenhão Sua apozentadoria, e Juizes e Officiais della e haja os ditos Uinte e quatro e tenhão os ditos expritais, e estem à Menza da Veriação da dita Cidade aSy a tão inteiramente Como tinhão e fazião antes da dita Sentença Contra ella Ser dada porquanto nossa mercê e Vontade he hauermos a dita Sentença por nenhuma e a dita Cidade, e Pouo della por dezoubrigado e releuado de tudo, o que dito he, e Como por a dita Cidade fazermos Mercê; Porem mandamos aos Veriadores della e a nosso Corregedor, Juizes, Justiças e Officiais e pessoas a que esta nossa Carta for mostrado e o Conhecimento por qualquer Guiza que seja pertencer que muy inteiramente a Cumprão e Guardem e fação Cumprir e Guardar aSy e na maneyra que Se nela Contem, Sem Contra ella hirem em parte alguma nem em todo, porque aSim he nossa mercê e nos praz Dada em a nossa Vila de Sintra a dous Dias do mez de Agosto Afonço Gomes a fez Anno de Nosso Senhor Jezus Christo de mil e quinhentos e Outo Annos não Seja duvida na entrelinha ahonde Diz noues nem dá per que se fez por Verdade Rey.

[signed] Esteuão Cardozo

— Franz-Paul Langhans, *A Casa dos Vinte e Quatro*, 171.